Ted Bundy

True Crime Stories of Murder
Homicide Horror and Evil

*(The Crimes and Life of One of America's Most
Infamous and Blood Thirsty)*

Bob Hines

Published By **Oliver Leish**

Bob Hines

All Rights Reserved

Ted Bundy: True Crime Stories of Murder Homicide Horror and Evil (the Crimes and Life of One of America's Most Infamous and Blood Thirsty)

ISBN 978-1-77485-863-9

No part of this guidebook shall be reproduced in any form without permission in writing from the publisher except in the case of brief quotations embodied in critical articles or reviews.

Legal & Disclaimer

The information contained in this ebook is not designed to replace or take the place of any form of medicine or professional medical advice. The information in this ebook has been provided for educational & entertainment purposes only.

The information contained in this book has been compiled from sources deemed reliable, and it is accurate to the best of the Author's knowledge; however, the Author cannot guarantee its accuracy and validity and cannot be held liable for any errors or omissions. Changes are periodically made to this book. You must consult your doctor or get professional medical advice before using any of the suggested remedies, techniques, or information in this book.

Upon using the information contained in this book, you agree to hold harmless the Author from and against any damages, costs, and expenses, including any legal fees potentially resulting from the application of any of the information provided by this guide. This disclaimer applies to any damages or injury caused by the use and application, whether directly or indirectly, of any advice or information presented, whether for breach of contract, tort, negligence, personal injury, criminal intent, or under any other cause of action.

You agree to accept all risks of using the information presented inside this book. You need to consult a professional medical practitioner in order to ensure you are both able and healthy enough to participate in this program.

TABLE OF CONTENTS

Introduction 1

Chapter 1: Beginning Years 4

Chapter 2: The Academic And Professional Life 9

Chapter 3: Pathology And Psychiatric Analysis 53

Chapter 4: At The Start Of The End Bundy's Initial Arrests.. 63

Chapter 5: He Is His Own Judge The Jury And Executioner..................................... 73

Chapter 6: Death Row The Decisions 77

Chapter 7: Victims' Family Involving Closure And Sentiments......................... 90

Chapter 8: The Arrest Trial And Escape Success 94

Chapter 9: Depths Of Wickedness........ 118

Chapter 10: The Birth Of Killer 143

Conclusion 182

Introduction

Theodore Robert Bundy is the most well-known serial killer of American history. The self-described "the most cruel boy one could ever come across" The saga of his brutal murders spans over two decades, and affected the lives of thousands of people, including the victims' families and family members. Following being born within Vermont, Bundy moved with his mother to Washington State- presumably under the assumption of being his sibling. A seemingly peaceful life as a child was followed a turbulent college years and relationships that did not have the commitment. The first time he was in a serious relationship, he was broken up by him when he realized that he did not have the maturity and dedication to his professional life that would allow him to be compatible with her ideal partner. Once the relationship was revived, Bundy exacted revenge by abruptly ending all contact and then shortly after began to unleash his anger on women of the area. He was able to commit numerous murders over the years due to a variety motives. He was well-educated, clean and well-dressed. Criteria that weren't in line with the ideals for criminals, according to authorities in law enforcement that were in place at the time. Bundy was seen among his prey as attractive and charming and utilized this advantage when making contact with them. He faked injury and identity in order to convince the victims to accept his pleas for assistance or cooperation. After taking them captive and overpowering them, he would then sexually attack and kill their victims in secondary places, then return to engage in sexual relations with their bodies, and make them dress in accordance with his own wishes. He decapitated a number of victims and put their bodies in home for weeks at one time. The manner of killing changed from being primarily driven by rage to ritualistic as he began to realize the control the victims he had. After his first arrest in Utah his time as a suspect who was elusive ended. The car he was driving had evidence that led investigators look for evidence that could be connected to other criminal acts. Following his arrest and conviction in Utah the accused was charged with murder in the case of a Colorado murder. Following an escape and capture, he was found guilty of murder within Colorado and was successful in another escape of longer time, in which he was convicted of his final trio of murders. This time, he was in Florida in which he was sentenced to the death penalty and was pronounced dead on the chair in 1989.

Chapter 1: Beginning Years

Born Theodore Robert Cowell, Theodore "Ted" Bundy entered life facing a massive social disadvantage. Bundy is a native of Burlington, Vermont to an unwed mother in the time it was considered inherently morally shady and unwise to be pregnant outside of the norm. The identity of his father is unknown, and the only details shared by his mother is of a sexually attractive encounter with a seaman identified as Jack Worthington.

Ted was raised in Vermont in a family home for mothers who were not married and later relocated to his grandparents' home in Philadelphia. The family believed that the stigma of being raised as an unlegitimate child could be too burdensome on the young Ted and they created the story that he was an adopted child, and claim that the mother of their son was his sister. Bundy was believed to have been a fan with his father, who was angry and was fond of pornography. There were signs of trouble before the end of the day for Bundy because it was reported that he was possessed of a bizarre obsession with knives from the age of three. An aunt has claimed that he gathered an assortment of knives in her kitchen as she slept.

A few years later, on the advice of his relatives, the mother of Ted, Eleanor Cowell, relocated along with Ted the family to Tacoma, Washington where they resided initially with their cousins. The following year, she was introduced to Johnny Culpepper Bundy at a church gathering. The following year, they were married and had many children. Their relationship with Bundy as well as his father was not characterized by any incident worthy of mentioning as well as there are no clear evidence that he was ever subjected to any kind of physical or mental assault in his home life. Many would think that Bundy was raised in a typical, working-class family.

If asked to remember details of the time that Bundy attended public school the majority of people said that his school days were those of a sociable kid who was surrounded by friends and excelled as an academic. This perception changed when

Bundy became a high school student. The confidence of Bundy began to fade as he began to withdraw and the acclaim of his junior high days vanished. He was awkward in social settings and his academic performance was not comparable to the previous years. This was confirmed by Bundy who said that he was incompetent when it comes to understanding the dynamics of interpersonal relationships, and not understand how to interact with people to establish friendship. This is why the majority of his time was in solitude during his adolescent yearsdue to his inability to be a healthy member of a group. He was branded an armed robber, and was arrested twice as a suspect in burglary as well as car theft towards the end in his high-school years. In the years prior to this, he was a keen skier, and was often able to satisfy his enjoyment of the sport with stolen equipment and fake lift tickets.

Bundy's teenage years were tainted with a myriad of undesirable behaviors however there are contradicting information about this as well as different aspects of his life with the information that are given to one individual are not in line with the information that were given to one. Some of his friends told him stories of scouring through garbage for pictures of naked women and scenes, as well as looking for magazines with crime stories that depict sexual violence, especially ones that included pictures of bodies that were killed or damaged bodies. This is a stance he refuted and completely denied to a different biographer. He claimed that he frequently had a large amount of alcohol in his drink and to have also searched for wide windows to be able to observe women while they were getting undressed or changed into bedding.

A subject that is a bit obscure or subject to debate is the moment in time when Bundy discovered the truth about his birth, as well as being aware that the mother of his was pretending to be his sister for years. When he was confronted about it during the time following the murder, Bundy gave conflicting accounts regarding the moment when he uncovered the truth. One story has him telling his girlfriend that a relative once called him"a "bastard" and then showing him the birth certificate. Another story has him telling several biographers that they found the birth certificate by himself. Some believe that he found the truth when he decided to look into the matter himself and, in 1969, he found the original birth certificate in Vermont.

Chapter 2: The Academic And Professional Life

After graduating of high school Bundy was accepted into the University of Puget Sound in 1965, where he spent a few days before transferring into University of Washington. University of Washington in 1966 where he decided to pursue Chinese. The following year, he came across an alumnus known as Stephanie Brooks with whom he began to develop an intimate relationship. Stephanie was attractive with dark, long hair, which was cut at the middle, a characteristic that was shared by a majority of Bundy's victims later on. The couple dated for a few years before Bundy quit Stanford to find low-wage employment and became active during 1968's Presidential campaign as an Nelson Rockefeller delegate. The impression that Bundy was lacking in commitment to his career and ambitions along with the perception that he was not mature enough was the reason that prompted Brooks to break up with him and move back with her parents. The breakup was devastating for

Bundy and was believed by many to be the moment in his life when Bundy began to seek out human outlet for the disappointments of his social ills. Bundy quit California and headed to the east, to visit family members in various places throughout the journey. He was a student studying at Temple University in 1969, and it is believed that it was during the time he began to find out the truth about the identity of his mother.

The former resident came back to Washington State in 1969 and started a friendship in 1969 with Elizabeth Kloepfer who was employed by the University of Washington School of Medicine. The relationship was volatile and lasted until his first prison sentence in the year 1976. He was able to re-enroll at the University of Washington in 1970 as a psychology major with more focus and direction than in previous pursuits at higher-education. His academic success earned him the status of an honor student and was held with respect by his teachers. His connection of Ann Rule began when the two were both volunteers at a suicide center. Rule was later worried after the profile of the police on this Pacific Northwest killer was made public and she offered an anonymous tip, but it was not taken seriously. Following his graduation in 1972, Bundy continued his political interests by assisting governor Daniel J. Evans' successful re-election campaign . In addition to that, he was employed for the position of assistant to the chairman of the Washington State Republican Party. In 1973, Bundy applied to law school and then in the fall, was accepted into University of Puget Sound. University of Puget Sound. The previous year, he had met up with Brooks and the two started having a relationship again. The topic of marriage was brought into conversation between them and she was introduced as his fiancee in front of some within his circle of political friends. In January 1974, their relationship came to an abrupt stop. Bundy was no longer meeting Brooks and was unable to respond to messages or phone calls. There was no explanation to explain why he stopped communicating. When he finally responded to the phone one month later, he provided no explanation or reason for why he decided to break up their relationship with no any explanation. The last communication that occurred between them. Bundy later said that he had planned to end their relationship once the time he believed it was possible to have married her in order to get revenge on her for breaking up with their relationship earlier. Following the end of their relationship, Bundy began to fade away from his law school pursuits and this is evident in his decreased attendance. About the time he was about to finish of his first year , he left the school completely and it was the start of a second disappearance of women in their teens who resided in the region.

Pattern and Process Modus Operandi of Ted Bundy

To be successful in avoiding arrest for a number of years of repeated brutal killings They must show an exceptional level of organization. They must also be able to comprehend the way authorities conduct investigations and attempt to catch the perpetrators. Bundy had this knowledge and knowledge in abundance. He faced law enforcement officials with numerous issues. It took several years and a number of victims before investigations conducted by independent investigators which were geographically based could establish a link and recognize that they were the same suspect. He decided to target his victims with techniques that reduced the chance of detection , as there was hardly any sound and no trauma, either by blunt force or strangulation- both that could have been accomplished by using any of the many things that were easily available in the majority of homes. The theory is that he surveyed the locations of his future abductions in a meticulous attempt to assess the level of danger and chance of committing the crime. He did not employ guns because of the obvious amount of noise, not to mention the remnants of ballistic evidence that could remain in the aftermath. He killed his victims by burning and removing their clothes in isolated locations with a minimal amount of activity from humans. His fingerprints have never been found on a crime scene which is remarkable considering the number of women killed by him throughout the years that can result from his keen attention to the smallest of details.

One pattern that was apparent with time was the distinct victim profile. The majority of victims were white females and the majority of them were between 15 and 25 , and many were in colleges which offered higher-education. They had never previously met Bundy in any way. Many had long, straight dark hair that was divided at the middle, a look identical to Stephanie Brooks who became an source of contention among Bundy and those who were analyzing the reasons behind his disgusting actions.

Another benefit that Bundy could make use of was the appearance that appeared to be erratic due to the capability of his facial expressions to alter his appearance so as to make the viewer question whether they were actually looking at the same person in several photos. Bundy made use of this attribute and would alter the way he cut or styled his hair to change the way he looked. his appearance. In order to cover the distinctive dark mole that hung from his neck, Bundy donned turtleneck sweaters and turtlenecks. Bundy was generally thought of as extremely attractive and well-groomed and was also known for his charming personality. He was confident and spoke with authority , which made the people whom he met follow his example.

Bundy's tactics evolved over time, adding social factors and other complication elements to his assaults. At first, Bundy would break into a house and quickly perform a brutal attack with an object that was sharp while the victim was asleep. One of the first victims was the ones who suffered a sexual assault that was so violent to cause severe physical harm to the genitalia and internal organs. This strategy was used again during the recent attacks that took place in Florida following his status as a wanted person was well-known.

In later years, he would employ more elaborate methods of luring his victims into situations which would allow him to subdue them and later capture them. At times, he would fake injury by using fake casts or crutches, and then solicit young women's their help to transport a briefcase, or any other object to his car or even request their assistance in the operation of his sailboat (which was not even in existence). In other instances , he pretend to be local officials (police security guards, police officers or firemen, etc.) and use an authoritative voice. If he can convince them to enter his car or even bring them near it, he might physically take them down, or give them a blow that could cause them to be unconscious and place handcuffs over them to secure the vehicle. Then came strangulation and/or sexual assault and/or strangulation, which could happen at the scene of the crime but most often occurred at the disposal site or another site in a faraway location.

The ritualistic act he performed included elimination of the clothing worn by his victim and then sexual encounters with dead bodies. He would dress and groom in clothes of his choice. It was noticed by relatives that the deceased didn't have or were not recognized to be wearing the items of clothing he dressed in. He would also paint nails with a color that was unrecognizable to people who were close to the victim.

Timeline of Victims

There's a lot of speculation as to when and how Bundy began to target women in his murderous spree. This creates uncertainty about the motives underneath his brutal behaviour. Bundy's personal narratives that he has shared during interviews of criminal psychology experts and experts are highly contradictory. One thing is that according to his statements that his first murder took place at the time of his murder in New Jersey only for him to later assert that he never killed anybody until two years afterward at Washington State. There is evidence that his first murder was before his breakup with Brooks that makes it more difficult for any attempt to comprehend his motives.

This is a list of Bundy victims as identified by confessions or evidence from the scene, which matches the description of his confessed murders throughout the decades. He once informed his investigators that there was certain murders he was not willing to speak about, and there were three criteria that he could not exclude: "too young", "too close to home" or "too close to family".

Name: Anne Marie Burr

Age: 8

Day of the Disappearance 13 August in 1962

Status: Unconfirmed - body never recovered

The girl's home was only 10 blocks to Ted Bundy, who was fifteen years old in the year. She was introduced to Bundy via his newspaper routes and often followed him when Bundy delivered newspapers. When she went missing, she went to her parents' room and informed their daughter was sick. The parents believed that she was in their bed but when they awoke next day, she was absent. The girl reportedly went out by a window that was open, dressed in bed clothes. A search conducted by the local police to nothing.

Name: Lonnie Trumbull

Age: 20

The Date and Time of the Homicide 23 June in 1966

Status: Confirmed - Murdered

Lonnie Trumbull was employed as Stewardess alongside their roommate Lisa Wick. After a night out with her boyfriend, around 10 pm, Lonnie and Lisa went to the bed. The next morning, their roommate returned home at 9:15 in the morning and found the front door to the house locked. She returned to their room , where she thought she'd be able to find them asleep and they were severely wounded. Lonnie was dead, however Lisa was spared the attack however, she was unable to remember anything when she awoke from the in a coma.

Susan Davis Susan Davis

Age: 19

Time of Appearance: May 30th 1969

Status: Confirmed - Murdered/Remains Recovered

Name: Elizabeth Perry

Age: 19

Time of Appearance: May 30th 1969

Status: Confirmed - Murdered/Remains Recovered

Davis as well as Perry were found murdered to death in Atlantic City, New Jersey during the time that Bundy was attending Temple University and lived in the vicinity. The bodies of the two were discovered within three days in a forest area. Strangely, one was naked and the other one was dressed in full. Bundy's links to the murders stem from the confession he made to an investigator that his first victim was a woman from the Philadelphia region.

Name: Rita Curran

Age: 24

Day of incident 19 July 1971

Status: Confirmed - Murdered

Curran was an elementary school teacher who was employed at an hotel located next to the house of the mother who was unwed that was where Bundy was born. The unmarried woman was practicing with her barbershop group until the end of the night and was last seen alive in her residence at around 11:15. The roommates returned later that evening the body was discovered naked and badly beaten. Her injuries were the hallmarks of the typical Bundy attack. She was strangled, beaten and raped, but after interrogation Bundy wasn't identified as suspect however, it was proven that Bundy was living in Vermont in the summer prior to the attack.

Name: Rita Lorraine Jolly

Age: 17

Date of Disappearance Date of Disappearance: June 29, 1973

Status Unconfirmed

Rita was last seen leaving the West Linn, Oregon residence to walk around 7:15 pm and has not been seen since. The last time she was seen just two hours after her departure walking down Sunset Avenue.

Name: Vicki Lynn Hollar

Age: 24

The Date and Time of Appearance 20 August in 1973.

Status Unconfirmed

Hollar had last been seen in her car on the morning of her disappearance, about 5pm on the night of her disappearance in Eugene, Oregon. She was supposed to meet with a person that evening to go to a local party however she did not show up. Bundy is the most likely possibility of being the cause for her disappearance even though Oregon authorities didn't have the chance to inquire regarding any possible connection prior to the execution. Her case is similar to the other victims he has and is confirmed to be located in the area when she went missing.

Name: Lynda Ann Healy

Age: 21

Date of Disappearance Date of Disappearance: January 31, 1974

Status: Confirmed - Murdered

Healy disappeared in the late morning on January 31st the 31st of January, 1974. A student in Washington State University, she was going about her usual routine that included classes and her job as an expert in ski forecasting. She fell asleep in the evening, as her friends returned to their homes later in the evening, they thought she was asleep. The next day, a alarm from her roommate went off and she noticed that Lynda's alarm was still ringing. She went into the room and shut it off only to discover it was bed already made which was a bit odd considering Lynda typically did not make her bed until next day. Lynda's boss contacted her to say that she'd not shown up for work. It was found that the bicycle that she usually rode to work was not located in the basement. The side door was discovered unlocked , and when her parents turned up for dinner they had promised her to prepare but she had not returned and the police were summoned. The police were in her bedroom and pulled up the sheets to find blood-stained sheets and a pillowcase stained by blood. Apart from her nightgown, which was tucked away in her closet There were no evidence of an attack or struggle. It wasn't until one year after her death when her body was discovered in what became known as Bundy's burial site. Her skull was badly crushed. The murder occurred after Bundy admitted to before being executed.

Name: Donna Gail Manson

Age: 19

Day of Appearance 12 March 1974

Status: Confirmed - Murder Confession

Manson disappeared on the 12th of March 1974, from Evergreen State College where she was an undergraduate student. Donna was especially susceptible to being exploited by Bundy because she regularly smoked marijuana and was often seen taking off with no warning and come back to tell her acquaintances about wild stories of traveling by hitchhiking. Because of her tendency to disappear for extended periods of time, she was unable to come back after having left for an event on campus, the disappearance of her was not made public until six days after. Her body was never discovered when she left her home at 7 pm. Bundy later admitted to the murder, declaring her body was among the ones found in the early months of March in Taylor Mountain, Washington.

Name: Susan Elaine Rancourt

Age: 19

The Date and Time of the Disappearance 17 April 1974

Status: Confirmed - Murder Confession

Susan had an unusual characteristic that was not shared by Bundy's other female victims of the young age she was blonde with blonde hair. She was a full-time student at Central Washington State College. In the evening, she vanished. she was seen leaving campus at dusk on April 17th, 1974 . She was scheduled to attend a conference for an opening in the job market for potential dorm advisors. The last time she was seen, she left the meeting of advisors and was planning to watch an German movie with her colleague but did not show up. The skull of her was the sole body part that was found nearly an entire year after her disappearance at Taylor Mountain. Bundy admitted she killed her before being executed.

Name: Roberta Kathleen Parks

Age: 20

Date of Disappearance Date of Disappearance: May 6, 1974

Status: Confirmed - Murder Confession

The murder of Kathy was doubly devastating for her family since the days before her disappearance on May 6, 1974, she was involved in an dispute with her father on the phone. The day she went missing, her sister called informing her of her father's heart condition however, she called back later to inform her of the news of a possible recovery. In the evening, she set out to visit the dormitory of a friend to have a cup of coffee, but she was not able to make it. Her remains were found among of the numerous bodies found in Taylor Mountain in early March of 1975. Bundy admitted to the murder prior to being executed.

Name: Brenda Carol Ball

Age: 22

The Date and Time of Appearance 1 June 1974

Status: Confirmed - Murder Confession

Ball had last been seen inside a tavern , where she was seen for a while through the wee dawn of June 1st 1974. Ball had last been seen with a male with an arm sling on the street in which she was parked. Her playful nature caused her people to take her absence serious - nobody was able to report her absent until 19 days after. On the 1st March of 1975, students from the college performing the work of Taylor Mountain discovered what was later discovered to be her skull. This was the first of many that were found in this area. The murder confession was signed to Ted Bundy prior to him being executed.

Name: Georgeann Hawkins

Age: 18

The Date and Time of Appearance 10 June in 1974.

Status: Confirmed - Murder Confession/Remains Recovered

Hawkins was a slim but a hardworking undergraduate at Washington University's Seattle campus. She contacted her mother on the 10th of June 1974, the date of her disappearance and informed her that she was working hard to study for her Spanish test the next day. After a night of partying she went to her boyfriend's bedroom to see him briefly before returning to her own bedroom to prepare to take your Spanish final. When she left the room of her boyfriend the next day, other acquaintances saw her on the street, where she was just 40 feet away from her final destination. If she didn't arrive within a couple of hours the roommate and boyfriend sought out the housemother in her dorm. She informed her that she was earlier awakened by an alarming scream. It was thought to be just the normal student scuffle outside of the dorms and was able to fall asleep. Bundy's confession of murder contained an unrequited recollection of how he found her be very trustworthy and sought her assistance in carrying his briefcase in reference to his faked accident and fake casting. She was willing to assist him, and he then fell unconscious, then she was thrown into his car before driving away. Before killing her she regained her consciousness and told him that she was sent to assist her in preparing for her Spanish test. He then knocked her unconscious with another brutal blow, and then strangled her in order to complete his grisly crime. Before being executed He testified to the fact that her remains were found on the 6th of September 1974 in the state park.

Name: Janice Ott

Age: 23

Date of Disappearance Date of Disappearance: July 14, 1974

Status: Confirmed - Murder Confession/Remains Recovered

Ott was a 23 year old probation caseworker from California who was devoted to helping people with personality disorders. Her job had brought her to Washington where she was unable to see her husband who was still living in Riverside, California at his own clinic. In the afternoon of her disappearance, she cycled through Lake

Sammamish State Park. Witnesses last saw her trying to assist a man who was in casts and could never be ever seen again. Her remains, as well as the remains of others were discovered in a location that was nearly two miles beyond the parks. A confession to murder came by Ted Bundy prior to his execution.

Name: Denise Naslund

Age: 18

Date of Disappearance Date of Disappearance: July 14, 1974

Status: Confirmed - Murder Confession/Remains Recovered

Naslund was a computer programmer, who was working part-time in order to pay for her way through college. Her boyfriend and she had been to Lake Sammamish State Park with other friends for a picnic in the afternoon. Denise was at the restroom facility around 4:30 and never returned. The dog was with her, turned up on her own. About two months after her death her remains were discovered on the same spot where the remains of victims were discovered nearly two miles away. Bundy admitted to murdering Naslund the day before he was killed Janet Ott in the same location.

Name: Nancy Wilcox

Age: 16

Day of Appearance 2 October 1974

Status: Confirmed - Murder Confession

Wilcox was missing from a neighborhood close to Salt Lake City, last seen as a passenger in an Volkswagen Beetle resembling that owned by Ted Bundy. Bundy admitted to murdering her prior to his death, and told the authorities her remains had been put in a remote location in the southwest of Salt Lake City.

Melissa Smith's Name Melissa Smith

Age: 17

The Date and Time of the Disappearance Oct 18 in 1974.

Status: Confirmed -Murder Confession/ Remains Recovered

Smith lived was a resident of Midvale, Utah- a tiny, tranquil Mormon community that the majority of residents would have believed to be a safe spot for a teenager to grow up with no apparent dangers. On the 18th of October Smith walked into an eatery in Midvale with a companion, and then she headed home to buy clothes for a night out. She didn't make it back home, and the body that was battered was found without clothing. Her head was brutally attacked with a massive metal object, perhaps an Crowbar. It was also discovered that she had been assaulted and strangled. Bundy made a confession to murder prior to his death.

Laura Aimee's Name Laura Aimee

Age: 17

Date of Disappearance The date of disappearance was October 31, 1974.

Status: Confirmed - Murder Confession/Remains Recovered

Aimee had a reputation as a unsecure high school dropout who gained the reputation of being an impulsive wanderer looking for her place in the world. The last time she was seen, she was in an establishment at night on Halloween, following which she walked off to an outdoor park. It was the last time anyone was observed of her. The body was discovered within a month of her death along an unnamed riverbank within the Wasatch Mountains. It was evident that her face had been badly bruised that she couldn't be identified through the use of her appearance. She was stripped of her clothing and beaten, strangled, sexually assaulted and beat by what appeared to be been a huge metal object. Bundy confessed that she killed her before being executed.

Name: Caryn Campbell

Age: 23

Date of Disappearance Date of Disappearance: February 12, 1975

Status: Confirmed - Murder Confession/Remains Recovered

Campbell lived at Farmington, Michigan and was traveling to Aspen along with her fiancée as well as his two children. She was engaged to a physician who was attending an event in town. the family decided it was a good idea to turn it into a holiday and so Campbell along with her two kids were invited along. While her fiancee attended an event, Campbell was taking the youngsters for a ski trip and explored. After dinner, the family went back to the hotel where they stayed for the duration of their stay. While the other guests were at the bar, Campbell returned to their room to find magazines and then disappeared for an unimaginably long length of time. Her fiancee searched for of her but to no avail. Police were called in, but they did not provide any evidence to be able to explain her disappearance. Her fiancée was forced to return to her home with her children, and he hoped for an explanation phone call but never received it. Six days after her disappearance, she was found dead. went missing, Campbell discovered dead in the snowbank just a few distance from the place which her party was staying. Police believed she was abducted within 30 yards of the entrance in her apartment. The woman was discovered naked, physically battered and with cuts. It was believed that she was sexually assaulted and raped. Bundy admitted to abduction and murder just prior to the execution that took place in Florida.

Name: Julie Cunningham

Age: 26

Day of Appearance 15 March 1975

Status: Confirmed - Murder Confession

Cunningham was a gorgeous young woman, who was believed to have experienced a challenging experience with romantic relationships. She was a victim of numerous heartbreaks, and the final one occurring within the same week that she would pass away. At the time of her disappearance, she talked with her mother one last time on the phone, and then headed to the local bar scheduled to see her friend however, she didn't show up. Bundy confessed to killing her right before his execution.

Name: Denise Lynn Oliverson

Age: 25

Day of the Disappearance 6 April 1975

Status: Confirmed - Murder Confession

Oliverson was another death that was tragic at multiple levels for relatives. Prior to her disappearance she had a heated debate with her husband. She then made the decision to ride off on her bicycle in order to see her parents. If she didn't come home, he figured there was a unresolved anger. He decided to wait for it to have time to settle and decided it was best for her to wait till the following day before calling the home of her parents. When he finally called at the time, he was surprised to discover that she had not turned to her home. Local law enforcement officials were contacted and found her bicycle and sandals under an overpass. A confession of murder received by Bundy before his death. In it, Bundy admitted that he put her body into the Colorado River which, swollen by snowmelt, could be carrying her body for miles downstream.

Name: Melanie Cooley

Age: 18

The Date and Time of Appearance 18 April in 1975.

Status: Confirmed - Murder Confession

The circumstances surrounding the disappearance of Cooley were similar to the circumstances of a few others Bundy victims. Cooley was a ranaway who had gone from her high school on the day she disappeared never to return. The body of her attacker was found just 20 miles away of the campus in an unmarked ditch. Her murder was confessed Bundy. Bundy before his execution.

Name: Lynette Culver

Age: 13

Date of Disappearance 6 May 1975

Status: Confirmed - Murder Confession

On the day of her disappearance Culver embarked on a trip to Fort Hall Indian Reservation outside Pocatello, Idaho, and she was never heard from ever again. A confession to murder received by Ted Bundy prior to his execution. He said he taken captive Culver and then taken her to the Holiday Inn where he raped her before drowning her in the tub. While it is believed that Bundy might have claimed credit for a few murders were not his and he also revealed details about Culver's past that he might get only from Culver's. He said that the moment he killed her she was buried into the Snake River.

Name: Shelly Robertson

Age: 24

Day of the Disappearance 1 July 1975

Status: Murder Confession Recovered

Following a dispute with her lover, Robertson went missing, and her friends didn't seem to be bothered by the incident, as she was subject to her own whims and was known for her traveling across states hitchhiking. In reality, weeks went by before her disappearance received adequate attention. The last time she was seen was made by a police officer who saw her at a petrol station, in the company of the driver of a decrepit truck. On the 21st of August, her body was discovered naked in the local mine. The decomposition rate prevented the identification of the cause of death. Her murder was admitted to Bundy prior to her execution. Bundy before his execution.

Name: Sue Curtis

Age: 15

Date of Disappearance Date of Disappearance: June 27, 1975

Status: Confirmed - Murder Confession

Curtis was kidnapped by a gang in Provo, Utah while attending an event located on campus at Brigham Young University. She had told her friends that she would walk for a quarter mile back to her dormitory in which she was staying to clean her teeth. After a thorough examination of her toothbrush by the authorities, they determined that she not returned to her room as her brush was dry. Bundy admitted to the murder of Curtis before being executed in 1989. The man claimed to dug her body in a highway close to the city of Price, Utah, but her remains have not been discovered.

Name: Debby Kent

Age: 17

The Date and Time of Appearance 8 November 1975

The night before the disappearance Kent was with parents see an athletic event in the school's auditorium after dropping her younger brother off at the rink for skating. When the play was over, Kent left. show Kent left her parents at school and set off to collect her brother. She did not make it to the skating arena. Residents living close to the school were reported to have heard two screams that were horrifyingly loud, however, other than walking out and look at the screams , they didn't do anything, even not calling authorities. The parents of the girl's distraught parents called the Bountiful police after all other vehicles had left the parking area and their daughter was still to come back. Witnesses told police they observed an uncolored Volkswagen Beetle leaving the school at a rapid speed.

Name: Debbie Smith

Age: 17

When the Date was Disappeared: Feb., 1976

Status: Confirmed - Remains Recovered

Smith's remains were found on April 1st, 1976 on the 1st of April, 1976 at Salt Lake International Airport.

Name: Lisa Levy

Age: 20

Date of Incident Date of Incident: January 14, 1978

Status: Confirmed - Murder

After returning from a disco on campus at 10:00 pm, Levy came home and went to her bed. She was the sole one in her dorm the evening, as her roommate was away to go on vacation. In spite of the chaos resulting from other assaults committed by Bundy on campus earlier in the day against Karen Chandler and Kathy Kleiner who both escaped with injuries that lasted for a lifetime, Levy was not apparently attentive. A police officer tried in bringing her back, however the effort was unsuccessful. A hairspray bottle was located in the vagina of her. The victim was injured by a bite to the right nipple which almost removed it out of her. Additionally the left collarbone of her been broken , and she may have died from strangulation. Bundy also left evidence on the scene of the attack, in the form of the bite wound that she suffered to her buttock. The evidence later assisted authorities in determine the identity of the perpetrator.

Name: Margaret Bowman

Age: 21

Date of Incident The date of the incident was January 14, 1978.

Status: Confirmed - Murdered

Bowman returned home after a blind date around the time of 9:30 and spent the last hours discussing the event with her fellow students at her residence. She fell asleep at about 2:30 am, and was found on her bed with her skull broken badly. A nylon stocking was tightly snared to her neck.

Name: Kimberly Leach

Age: 12

The Date and Time of the Disappearance 9 February of 1978.

Status: Confirmed - Murdered/Remains Recovered

Leach was missing from the junior high shortly after having left a class to go to her purse, which she hidden in her homeroom class. The teacher let her and a companion to return for it, and the other noting something she was looking to find, and leaving Leach alone. The next time the friend returned, she observed Leach walking away from the group with an adult male whom witnesses have reported as appearing angered. It was speculated that this was possibly an adult disciplining a disruptive child who was taken to home for the entire day. School officials realized there was something wrong and called the parents to inquire as to the reason she was not thoroughly checked out, and also why she hadn't attended any class. After being contacted by her parents, they knew that something was wrong since her the delinquency in school was uncommon for her. The absence of any evidence of her was to be seen when an exhaustive search was launched until her bones were discovered after 8 weeks in the pigpen. It was interesting that she was the only victim who didn't receive head injuries however there were indications of physical assault as well as strangulation.

The survivors of Bundy's Attacks

There were numerous instances where Bundy didn't finish his murder regardless of the reason. In some instances Bundy believed that the victims had died when they were rendered unconscious. Bundy is considered to be the main suspect or the main suspect in these attacks since the evidence and victims correspond to the profiles of other victims who confessed to him. In other cases it is possible that he was afraid due to the sound of other people coming within close to him. Nearly all of them suffered permanent injuries that typically involved brain injury and usually the genital region is damaged. This is a listing of survivors who have been identified:

Name: Karen Sparks

Age: 18

Date of Attack 4 February 1974

Sparks was asleep in the basement room in the shared rental house at the night before and the following day, she was found to have redness on her face as well as blood splattered on her hair. A rod made of metal that was part of the bed frame had been pushed up in her vagina. There was no memory of the assault.

Name Carol DaRonch

Age: 18

The date of attack: 8 November 1974

DaRonch was spotted by Bundy in the Waldenbooks shop at Salt Lake City, Utah. Bundy approached her, claiming to be an official informing her that her vehicle was taken away and that she was required to visit the scene and investigate the scene. DaRonch was, admittedly, naive on several fronts. Bundy asked her for she was using for her driver's license, instead of handing it over and she was not able to consider how he could find her since she had no prior relationship to her that could have provided him with some idea as to the physical appearance of the owner of the vehicle. His authority and confidence led her to believe that he was a security person and when she requested ID , he turned down the request with a sarcastic smile. They arrived at the vehicle in which nothing seemed to have gone missing. The suspect then demanded she accompanying her towards the "station" in order to assist in identifying the suspect. She made the choice to take her Volkswagen so that she could go towards the "headquarters" where the suspect was taken. She was advised to fasten her seat belt and refused to do. She was about to get from the vehicle, but at that point, she was able to get away and was quickly able to reach a rapid speed. He was traveling to the opposite end of the station of police when it came to a screeching stop and tried to put handcuffs around her. He erroneously put both wrists in cuffs while they fought. He then pulled out a gun as a threat to shoot her but she fell from the door, and he swarmed her with the Crowbar. He grabbed her, and then slung her against the vehicle however, presumably because of the power of pure adrenaline , she escaped and fled in the fastest speed possible to the highway, which a car was passing by at the right time. The car's driver drove Bundy to the station, where information from her case will later prove crucial for Bundy's arrest.

Another potential victim claims that they have escaped the clutches from Ted Bundy. In 1974, 21-year-old Rhonda Stapley was awaiting an appointment on a bus when Bundy approached her and offered an opportunity to take her within the back of his Volkswagen Beetle. She said he was "the neighbor boy" and maintained that he looked "normal" in that "he fit right in with the local community." Stapley accepted his invitation and , after he was in, Bundy got on the interstate and made an exit, and then left the highway in a remote location. He was chatting with Stapley, and then suddenly quieted down, at which point he muttered "You do you know what? I'm thinking I'm going to end your life." Then he began taking a bite out of Stapley who has claimed to have lost and then regained consciousness several times. Stapley was able to escape after arriving the final time and seeing Bundy in front of his car looking for something. The adrenaline kicked in, and she jumped up and ran away, eventually falling into a stream that took her downstream as she escaped her adversaries. When more girls from the area disappeared despite the desire to share her details, Stapley did not speak up. She was afraid that coming out would alert the criminal that authorities were on the lookout of him. She was also afraid to stand up for herself. It wasn't until 2011, following encouragement from her family that she sought out therapy and decided to come forward. It is important to note that some people have challenged her claims and believe that Stapley attempts to capitalize on Bundy's actions for financial gain in the form of advertising a book called"I Survived Ted Bundy and is doing interviews on People and the Dr. Phil show.

Name: Karen Chandler

Age: 21

Day of the Attack: January 14th in 1978.

Name: Kathy Kleiner

Age: 20

Day of the Attack: January 14th January, 1978

Chandler Kleiner and Kleiner were assaulted in their bedroom shortly at around midnight. The suspect, believed as Bundy has been observed by a person who witnessed the incident as he fled the house. The housemother was alerted by residents and discovered the two women very bloody and suffering numerous injuries. They were unable to provide any evidence of evidence due to their lack of memory.

Name: Cheryl Thomas

Age: 21

The date of attack: 15 January 1978

Thomas likely escaped the attack since Bundy was able to hear people coming too close to be comfortable. She was found in her bed, with numerous skull injuries and concussions. She also had nerve injury, a dislocated shoulder and a fractured jaw.

Bundy as a Suspect or Person Inquiring

There are some cases that do not match the Bundy profile in light of the evidence available or the testimony of witnesses, however his involvement in the case has not completely been eliminated. The following cases fall in this group:

Name: Joyce LePage

Age: 21

Date of Disappearance The date of disappearance was July 22, 1971.

Status: Confirmed - Murdered/Remains Recovered

LePage disappears from Washington State University where she was an undergraduate student. Her remains were found 9 months after her disappearance, encased in a carpet and tied by rope, in a forest ravine close to Pullman, Washington. Authorities tend to believe that Bundy is still an unsolved case.

Name: Sandra Jean Weaver

Age: 19

The Date and Time of Appearance 1 July 1974

Status: Confirmed - Murdered/Remains Recovered

Weaver was an habitant in Tooele, Utah whose nude body was found on the same day as her disappearance in a place close to Grand Junction, Colorado.

Name: Carol Valenzuela

Age: 20

The Date and Time of the Disappearance 2 August in 1974.

Status: Confirmed - Murdered/Remains Recovered

Name: Martha Morrison

Age: 17

Day of the Disappearance 1 September in 1974.

It is believed that the remains of Valenzuela along with Morrison were discovered in a grave that was shallow in the early part of October in Olympia, Washington. Bundy remains a suspect since the evidence suggests that he been on a journey across the state of Washington from Seattle from Seattle to Salt Lake City in August and may have traveled the route that involved

Vancouver and Eugene although this is purely speculation.

Name: Nancy Baird

Age: 23

Date of Disappearance Date of Disappearance: July 4, 1975

Status Unconfirmed

Baird was an attendant at a gas station in Layton, Utah. She often interacted with customers she didn't know, and was exposed to people she did not know working in an environment that carries an above-average danger of being victimized.

Chapter 3: Pathology And Psychiatric

Analysis

Bundy accepted to undergo numerous clinical examinations by experts from various institutions. The conclusions derived from the evaluations varied between the experts. One of the most frequent conclusions was that of several individuals. This was based on information provided in court interviews and testimony from relatives and justice officials. Bundy was said to have the capability to change identities to another, or at other times, simply appear as someone an person watching did not recognize.

The most convincing evidence for the diagnosis was that Bundy had an antisocial personality disorder, or ASPD. These individuals, frequently called "sociopaths" as well as "psychopaths" exhibit an outward appearance of socially acceptable qualities and appear to be sociable people however underneath they are unable to discern which is right from wrong, or don't have the capacity to experience guilt or remorse.

Bundy did not believe in the value of guilt, and acknowledged that guilt was never something was present at any point in his life. Other traits of sociopathic character which were displayed by Bundy included narcissism, lack of judgement and manipulative behavior. One of Bundy's psychiatrists acknowledged that Bundy used to manipulate him during his examination.

An interview with evangelicalist James Dobson of the Christian advocacy group Focus on the Family, Bundy claimed that pornography was the main cause behind his behaviour. He said that exposure to pornographic material can create an craving for sexual encounters that increases in degree of severity and aggression. Then, he stated that pornography was not able to satisfy the desire it instigated and that acting upon violent sexual desires was the only satisfaction he experienced. Although he did have others who were similarly concerned concerning the risks of pornography, such as Dobson however, others believe that it was just an attempt to shift responsibility and blame from him onto others. This was consistent that was common to Bundy who was to attribute blame on some other person or entity. Bundy could've avoided death penalty by assuming the responsibility for over 30 killings that he admitted prior to trial in Florida however he chose not to. He claimed that his life was unfair to him from the time of his birth to his early years, which includes the fact that he didn't have a actual father as well as the falsehood regarding his parents' ancestry. He also stated that the media, the police and alcohol were the culprits. TV and crime magazines were also a part of the problem. He even blamed the victims of his crimes for their vulnerability and said they facilitated the abuse.

Bundy did not appear to be motivated to play a game of cat and mouse game with the police or performing tricks on investigators while he continued to increase his number even though he wanted to avoid being arrested. There was no clear understanding of the extent of the crime he committed with regard to the lives he had affected. He seemed to only be striving to satisfy his desire to control the fate of other people. Serial killers are believed to build walls that are nearly impervious to their guilt. This is why it was difficult to extract confessions from Bundy because they required him to overthrow an enormous barrier that was erected in him from a long time ago.

The one thing that seemed to be relevant in any circumstance in the life of Bundy was that Bundy was the one in charge. This is evident by the way the victims he controlled, prior to and following the murder. They would be dressed according to his own taste and recreate scenes from crime magazines. In court the judge could not be more focused on the things that were most beneficial to ensure he had the best chance to get the highest possible verdict. It was only important that he stated whatever came to mind, and resisted surrendering the control of his actions, which included confessions that could have delayed his demise.

Live On The Kill

From January 4th until the beginning of in May Bundy began a killing spree throughout the Pacific Northwest that created tremendous tensions in the community and left police in a state of confusion on what they can do to stop the murders. Police and detectives of within the Seattle region were disappointed because there was no physical evidence aside from the typical appearance and traits of the victims. The murders continued, and law enforcement officers would carefully examine the scene of crime and find no evidence.

In a way, Bundy was employed by an agency called the Washington State Department of Emergency Services which took part in the search for missing women, however, no one in the agency saw enough reason to inquire. It was at this location that he came across Carole Anne Boone, who played a significant part in the final stage in his existence.

Television and newspaper coverage of the missing victims as well as the brutality of the crime scenes were awe-inspiring in both states in which the victims were. The fear of being a victim led to a decrease in female hitchhikers and public pressure was growing as the perception grew to be that police were not doing enough to catch the culprit.

The hands of police were bound as they were not able to divulge information that could compromise the investigation.

There was a growing number of commonalities in the victims. Abductions took place after dark, often near construction sites. The exact time was set to midterm or final examinations where many victims were students at college. Every victim was found to be wearing jeans or slacks. The majority of the time the picture of the suspect seen at the scene of the crime was one of a male driving in a Volkswagen Beetle with his arm in cast , or with a strap.

Police put out fliers that contained sketches of the composite and also published the flier newspapers, and then broadcast it on TV. Then, shortly after, Elizabeth Kloepfer, Ann Rule, a fellow worker from Bundy's work at DES and an University of Washington professor recognized the sketch, profile and vehicle, leading them to identify Bundy as a possible suspect.

Elizabeth Kloepfer met Bundy in 1969, and the two started dating. The turbulent relationship lasted seven years. Kloepfer eventually called police and spoke about what she believed to be unusual behavior from Bundy which was identical to the behavior of the murderer. She also told officers that Bundy was out frequently in the evening and that she was not sure exactly where he went or what he was doing during those hours. She also said that she had found items that she was unable to comprehend. Bundy was carrying an tool called a lug wrench as well as a set crutches, an Oriental knife and the meat cleaver. Additionally, she highlighted the similarity of Bundy and the sketch released by police however, police were not convinced the evidence she presented was enough to draw focus to Bundy as a possible suspect.

Rule met Bundy in 1971 when they were both on the hotline for suicide. Bundy and Rule volunteered and counseled the callers. They quickly became friends and she recalled his bringing her coffee. Local politicians, including The District Attorney were aware and praised him. Rule herself was a bit obsessed with him, even going to the extent of suggesting that had he been a bit younger, she would have been happy with her daughter being with him. The year 1974 was when Rule started her career as an investigative reporter in the region . She began to follow the series of murders and attempting to provide relevant reports. She was informed that witnesses was able to hear the suspect call himself "Ted" in addition to the fact that the police believed that he was driving an Volkswagen Beetle. Rule was unsure regarding this particular detail but the description generally matched Bundy in her memories of her time on the suicide hotline and she contacted an officer who was a friend of hers. When the officer contacted her she was informed that Bundy actually was the owner of the Volkswagen. Rule's tips were ignored by the police as Bundy continued to murder.

In the month of August 1974 Bundy received a second invitation to University of Utah Law School and transferred away from Seattle in the state of Washington to Salt Lake City. Within a matter of one month, he was murdering once more. In November, there were numerous young women who were reported missing in cities in the close vicinity to Salt Lake City. Kloepfer made contact with police King County police again and was interrogated by the detective. The status of Bundy as a suspect began to change, but the most reliable witness was unable to separate Bundy out of a photograph list. Kloepfer made a third call and this time at the Salt Lake County Sheriff's Office and gave an anonymous tip. There was no evidence to connect him to missing people in Utah however nothing further was done except to include him on the suspect list. In the month of January 1975 Bundy came back for a visit with Kloepfer from Seattle and stayed for a time with Kloepfer for a week. She arranged to visit Kloepfer during the month of Salt Lake City in August.

The focus of Bundy's killings moved eastward towards Colorado. Between January 12 and April 6, Bundy murdered three women across the state, and added another victim to his monthly total with 12-year-old Lynette Culver, who was from Pocatello, Idaho. He continued to have conversations with his acquaintances and friends and many of those who knew him were beginning to suspect of their involvement in the disappearances and killing of the many young women, who were increasing in numbers. In May, he was visited by Salt Lake City by three of his former colleagues at the Washington State DES, including Carole Ann Boone. Bundy returned to stay for one month with Kloepfer in Seattle together with Kloepfer in June, and they started discussions about getting married, despite being aware that Bundy was engaged in a continuous affair with Boone and was also dating an Utah lawyer.

In the meantime, Washington State authorities were trying to get better at analysing a massive amount of data, using a huge payroll computer operated by King County. After hours of tedious data inputs, they consulted the computer and it produced four lists of 26 names that were common to all One of them is Ted Bundy. The more and more indications pointed to Bundy.

Chapter 4: At The Start Of The End Bundy's

Initial Arrests

On the 16th of August 1975, an Utah Highway Patrol officer saw Bundy speeding through a residential area during the early morning time. When the patrol car was spotted, Bundy took off at the speed of light and the officer chased him and then arrested him. A search through Bundy's Volkswagen produced a couple of items including masks, an crowbar trash bags, handcuffs rope as well as an ice pick, among other items that could be utilized in burglaries. The description and call were relayed to dispatchers the suspect's vehicle, the description sounded like something that could be an investigator based on the details from the DaRonch kidnapping of the previous year. Detectives also remembered Kloepfer's contact information in her phone call from the prior month in December. A search of the Bundy's home revealed a map of Colorado ski resorts and an unidentified checkmark on that of the Wildwood Inn where Caryn Campbell was abducted. It also led to a booklet featuring that Viewmont High School play in Bountiful which Debra Kent had last been seen in. The evidence was considered persuasive, but not to the point of being incriminating. Following interrogation and a investigation, Bundy was released.

Bundy was placed under 24 hour watch for 24 hours by Salt Lake City police and three detectives flew into Seattle to speak with Kloepfer. They were told of her discovery that she discovered a number of mysterious items inside the house, which included crutches (Bundy did not have an injury that necessitated their use) as well as an unopened bag of plaster from Paris as well as an axe for meat that was not employed to cook with, gloves made of surgical an Oriental knife, as well as a vast number of women's clothing. She also gave an account of Bundy getting angry when confronted with a new stereo and television, and the threat that he would "break the neck of her" when she revealed the news to anyone. She also said that Bundy began to become "very unhappy" when she mentioned the possibility of cutting her hair, which she cut between the ears. He also displayed bizarre behavior while in bed when he was looking through the cover, taking a look at her body. He had an lug wrench inside the car's trunk, which was coincidentally (or not) with a Volkswagen Beetle, which he often borrowed "for security". An additional interview with another investigator revealed the connection with Bundy as well as Stephanie Brooks.

In September Bundy offered his car for sale to the Midvale resident, and it was later confiscated by Utah police. It was dismantled and sifted to find by FBI and they found hair that was found to match the sample from Caryn Campbell's body. Hair strands from other hairs were found to be the hair of Melissa Smith and Carol DaRonch. A brief assessment made by a federal laboratory specialist stated that the existence of hair strands within one vehicle that matched three distinct victims who never had the chance to meet the other was "a random coincidence of mind-boggling rareness".

Bundy was put in a line prior to Carol DaRonch who immediately identified him as the person who walked up to her, posing as a security guard in an attempt to lure her into the position of abducting her. The incident led to him being accused of aggravated kidnapping as well as attempted assault. He was also identified by witnesses for being the unidentified person in the auditorium at the high school but there was no sufficient evidence to link his disappearance with Debra Kent's missing.

After being helped through his parents' $15,000 loan, Bundy was able to live the majority of his time in Seattle being a visitor at the house of Kloepfer. He was under strict supervision under the watchful eye of Seattle police. In the time between his release and the trials for DaRonch kidnappings, a number of police officers from five states gathered to discuss the case in Aspen, Colorado. They were able to conclude that they were the ones responsible but that they did not have enough evidence to justify an indictment of murder.

Bundy was in the courtroom in February in 1976. He was charged with being involved in DaRonch kidnapping. According to his attorney, he renounced his rights to go through a trial by jury and the judge was found guilty of the assault and kidnapping charges. The judge sentenced him to up to 15 years of imprisonment in the Utah State Prison system. In October, being found in bushes possession of weapons that could help him escape, he was put in the solitary confinement. The that same time, he also was arrested for Caryn Campbell's death by Colorado authorities. He was then sent to Aspen in the month of January in the year following.

A Man who is a challenge to keep Up with - Bundy's escapes

Bundy was picked up on June 7, from a temporary detention facility and taken to his County Courthouse located at Aspen for his initial hearing. Despite his charges brought against Bundy Judges in this case didn't have him wear leg shackles or handcuffs. Bundy demanded to go to the library at the courthouse to look into his case. By using a bookcase as a cover for his body, he jumped from a windowsill on the second story , resulting in a broken ankle. He threw off his clothes and walked around Aspen and climbed Aspen Mountain. He smashed into a couple of recreation camping structures and began to wander around the mountain, but unable to locate the place he wanted to go. He was able to evade authorities who were looking for him up to the 6th of July when the car he was driving stolen and started weaving through the and out of his lanes. Police stopped and pulled Bundy over, who was experiencing sleep deprivation. He was detained.

When he was remanded to prison, Bundy began to play the worst of enemies for himself, as he refused to remain in prison and wait for his trial. The evidence was in favor of the acquittal of Bundy as the pretrial motions were ruled in his favor and certain pieces of evidence were found to be not admissible. Acquittals in Colorado could have deterred other prosecutors from pursuing charges without evidence which was difficult to obtain. There was a chance that Bundy would have regained freedom in less than 2 years left to serve on the DaRonch conviction.

Walking lightly does not seem to be a good idea for Bundy and so, instead of playing with a safe option, he decided to think of a different strategy for escape. Utilizing an outline of the floor of the jail as well as an axe and a hacksaw, he identified the location the exact location he required to cut a 1-foot square gap between the reinforcement bars on the ceiling. After a significant weight loss and a lot of effort, he managed to squeeze it through an area that was crawling. Following completion of the job of making holes, Bundy did exercises in order to get familiar with the facility. The night prior to New Year's Eve Bundy was successful in taking advantage of the fact that there was a smaller than usual number of jail personnel. This allowed him to go into the crawl space, and then drop into the ceiling of the apartment of the chief jailer that was empty since the chief jailer had gone out with his family members to celebrate the evening. Bundy took a few street clothes out of the closet of the jailer and then went to walk out of the entrance of the jail and make a second escape.

Bundy took a car which sadly for him, failed to start up at Interstate 70. He was taken care of by a driver who passed by and was taken to Vail which is where he took the bus to Denver. After that, he took a flight to Chicago. It was only after 17 hours the escape route was discovered within Glenwood Springs. Bundy left Chicago to Ann Arbor, Michigan by train. He watched the Rose Bowl contest between the Wolverines and his former school that is, that of the University of Washington, at the local bar. After five days, he took the car and drove to Atlanta. In Atlanta the bus he took headed to Tallahassee which he reached on January 8th. Bundy contemplated escaping the shackles of his past and pursue a career that would pay the bills and avoiding further crimes of violence. The odds were high of being unnoticed in the event that he didn't take any action that would draw the attention of police. He was unable to work on an industrial site when the police asked him to show proof of identity and reverted to his routine of stealing for his expenses.

The act of stealing was not the only vice he was reverting to. After being in town only for two weeks, Bundy entered Florida State University's Chi Omega sorority house at approximately 2:45 am. He then attacked four students in less than 15 minutes, probably within the ears of at least 30 students who claimed they didn't hear anything. On his next visit, Bundy left evidence of incrimination of his attack against Cheryl Thomas, as police took hair samples and semen later found to match to Bundy's. Unfortunately, Bundy was not finished. On February 8, Bundy took a van belonging to a university and drove it to Jacksonville. He tried to kidnap the 14-year-old however, his attempts were blocked by their older brother. He travelled towards Lake City that afternoon where he kidnapped 12-year-old Kimberly Leach from a school campus. He then killed she, committed suicide by throwing her corpse in a pig facility located just 35 miles to the west.

Bundy took the decision to Bundy decided to leave Tallahassee the 12th of February, and set off west across the Panhandle region. On February 15, he was detained by an Pensacola police officer near the Alabama state line, following an identification check showed that the Volkswagen Beetle was reported stolen. When he was informed that he had been detained, Bundy knocked the policeman's legs off of his and then fled. A physical confrontation among Bundy and the officer concluded by Bundy being subdued and being taken into custody. The car that was stolen contained an abundance of evidence that could be used in the trial, including IDs of three Bundy's FSU sorority members, as well as the mask he wore as he attempted to abduct the Jacksonville teenager.

Chapter 5: He Is His Own Judge The Jury

And Executioner

When Bundy was charged with the murders and assaults of those who were Florida State University sorority members Bundy's repute as a violent criminal was rapidly growing. The court trial, later moved to Miami and telecast throughout the nation on television. There were more than 250 news reporters. including many from other nations, were present for the proceedings of the court.

The majority of defendants who are facing trial for multiple murders which could lead to their being sentenced to death row, are generally content to follow the counsel of their lawyer. Most of the time, they will plead according to the procedure advised by their lawyer and are able to avail any plea bargain that could be made, as it is their chance to stay clear of the death penalty. Bundy chose to take the opposite strategy, one that seemed to have took defeat out of the face of victory.

In the same way that Bundy didn't listen to the suggestions of professionals and friends while he was in detention in Utah and was later released, he adopted the same approach with regard to being tried and facing the accusations that he was charged with in Florida. The defense team of his client had reached an agreement to plead guilty the exchange of his admission and plea bargain to three murders, Bowman, Leach, and Levy and Levy, he could get out of the death penalty and instead get 75 years of prison. This could do more than stay out of the death penalty because after a period of time been passed and witnesses had died or had lost the ability to recall specific details, it was possible to file an appeal that would result in an Acquittal. All the pieces were in place to allow for this scenario, but Bundy took the decision at the end of the day to refuse the plea. The public defender for the case of Mike Minerva, believed that it was an unimaginable admission of guilt Bundy could not get over in order to take the plea.

Bundy's choice quickly led to his death due to the evidence against his case. An Chi

Omega sorority member identified Bundy as the solitary person she observed around the area of the house on that night of the attack. Another witness claimed to have seen Bundy walk out of the sorority home with the weapon used in the murder. Forensic dentists confirmed that the dental impressions of Bundy's were in line with bite marks made on the buttock of Lisa Levy. Deliberations took less than 7 hours before the court pronounced a verdict on the 24th of July in killings committed by Bowman and Levy and three charges of attempted first degree murder as well as two burglary charges. The murder convictions led to being sentenced to death.

Bundy was tried six months later, accused of abducting and murdering Kimberly Leach. The trial took just eight hours before an indictment of guilty was issued. The most important evidence in his favor was the witness testimony from an eyewitness who saw him driving Leach into his van that was stolen. There was also evidence of fibers found in Bundy's coat that were similar to the ones found in his vehicle, as well as an analysis of Leach's body. A further bizarre development was that Bundy made an engagement proposal to his former colleague in the Washington State DES, Carol Ann Boone. Boone had relocated to Florida to have a closer relationship with Bundy she testified on behalf of Bundy in both trials. There was a little-known Florida law states that a marriage certificate in an official court before an official judge is a valid marriage. Boone agreed and Bundy announced before the judge that they had become married and were. The jury was not likely to show much compassion for the newlyweds when Boone was sentenced to the third time he was sentenced to death on Feb 10 in 1980.

Chapter 6: Death Row The Decisions

Following his death sentence, issued, the lengthy appeals process that ran for several years, started. Bundy was interviewed by a variety of people during this time as well as others upon his request, and others from those seeking to learn more about the thought processes and thoughts of the serial killer. Bundy was even consulted for assistance in helping investigators solve other related murders which bear the hallmarks of serial killers.

One of the first things Bundy confirmed was that his habits and conduct as a thief were the primary reason for him to acquire the majority of his items and how that he satisfied his demands. He claimed that he stole items primarily for an illusion of ownership and the sense of ownership. By taking something and declaring it as the sole possession of his gave him higher feeling of ownership that if he taken it in a honest manner. This was extended to those who were the victims of his attacks. The killings were initially carried out because of necessity, so that it would not be caught.

The sexual assaults he performed on his dying victims, or the necrophilia-related acts committed against the bodies allowed him to obtain "total ownership" of the victims. This was the reason for his desire to go home with skulls, and his subsequent to the sites of decomposition where he dressed the dead in clothes of his choice or painted their nails. Bundy in a separate interview spoke about the way in which victims become part of his. Both the murderer as well as the victim are one. The sites which he left were sacred places, and he longed to visit them again to experience the same thing again. Bundy spoke of a change in the manner of his murder with terms such as "impulsive" as well as "amateur" for the murder of his beginnings, followed by his transformation to "prime" as well as "predator" status in 1974.

Bundy will go on to describe in terrible details how he went about abducting, brutally attacking the victims and torture them. He claimed that he threw the skull of one of his victims to the flames of his close friend Elizabeth Kloepfer. He elaborately explained how he enticed, subdued and assaulted the victim, and then stayed the night in her body. He then visited the body at three separate times. Bundy's testimony proved to the police pathologists who examined him that he had been obsessed with murder the entire time. His crimes were committed with complete disdain, showing a rage at women that came from deep within , and never relented. He said he would bring Utah victims to his home "where it was possible to reenact the scenes that were depicted on the cover in detective books."

A new motive was revealed during the interviews and interrogations with officials within Utah as well as Colorado. Bundy seemed to be trying to get a stay of execution by omitting information and asserting that there were other victims who weren't recognized. Authorities offered no evidence in this case because the information offered did not provide any additional information, and in most instances , there was no new information or evidence was discovered. A detective interpreted this act to avoid execution by Bundy as a clash between his attempts to avert execution, while not releasing the "total ownership" of the victims by divulging the holy burial site of their remains, which was something only he had.

Confessions and New Information

After all his pleas had been exhausted, and with no reason to deny the terrible acts the man had done, Bundy chose to speak with investigators in search of the solution to many unsolved cold cases and murders. Bundy was the principal suspect in eight murders that occurred in Washington and Oregon and made a confession. He offered information that led to the disappearances of three more people from Washington and two others in Oregon. There were additional deaths within Idaho, Utah and Colorado that the authorities were not aware about. As a last effort to negotiate the issue of a stay of execution Bundy supporters urged relatives of some members of Colorado as well as Utah victims to intervene and ask the Florida Governor to postpone the execution which would allow Bundy to reveal more details which could lead to repatriation and burials of loved family members. The families did not agree, citing the belief that the victims died and that Ted Bundy was responsible. From their point of view the only person who could gain anything from the incident was Ted Bundy.

It's the Hunt For The Green River Killer

On a hot summer day in 1982, the two first bodies of a series of murders that wouldn't be solved for more than more than two decades were discovered along the banks of the Green River. In the end, Gary Ridgway would confess to more than 40 murders, the victims being street-walkers and prostitutes whom he believed were a waste of time who no one would want to be able to ignore. He was able to escape the authorities investigating the cases of missing persons , and then murder victims when their remains were found.

In the month of October in 1984, Detective Robert Keppel was trying to sort through the pile of papers on his desk when a different detective came in and handed him an unsigned letter to an order of a judge. The letter was written by someone who offered a an opinion regarding The Green

River killings that had caused the most recent controversy in the Seattle region. The letter came sent by Ted Bundy, a fact that shocked Keppel. Keppel and a Detective, Dave Reichert, discussed the issue and decided that they would have nothing to lose by speaking to Bundy who could possibly give an insight into the thoughts of serial murderers, and help them understand the steps required to stop them. There were a series of meetings that followed and Bundy was able to identify the suspect of the Green River killings as "the riverman." Bundy conveyed some of his behavior towards his victims as he explained the investigators who were visiting that it was crucial to locate a new body in the event that one turned to be found. The suspect would likely return to the location to have a sex session with the corpse, or have a conversation with the person they had sole possession of following the murder.

Reichert discovered she observed that Bundy and Ridgway had a few traits in common. They both seemed to have a facade of slickness and intelligence but in reality, the core, they were both sad uncaring and not arousing. Both were hunter-gatherers seeking control and control over their victims. There was no regret for the harm done to the victims and there was no deep feelings that could be measured towards family members or people who could at first glance be considered friends considering the length of time they spent with them.

What made Bundy's Apprehension Last So Long?

There are many elements and aspects that make an investigation into a serial killer The most important one is that it takes lengthy time (and many murders) before you can conclude that a mass killer is to deal with. In the case of Bundy's it was revealed that he killed eight women before authorities pondered the idea that they might have had a repeat killer with their hands. There were months before missing person cases turned into homicide investigations, when remains were discovered and the authorities were informed. It gives an opportunistic killer similar to Bundy who has no other motives apart from the desire to kill and accumulate possessions time to commit murder again and again. When police from the Pacific Northwest were zeroing in on Bundy He was already killing at least in Utah in addition to Colorado.

This issue isn't specific to this particular case, but is certainly evident when murders occur in multiple jurisdictions and involve a number of agencies that are charged with the responsibility of capturing the suspect and resolving the crime. It's collaboration and coordination. When the murders were committed in the Seattle region and in the Oregon region there were more than five agencies involved at the time of the incident. Apart from being separated due to distance and physical boundaries, there was also communication problems. Each police department had its own procedures and priorities. The latest information about developments was not communicated to all agencies in the same time. Lack of uniformity was evident in the manner that different agencies carried out investigation, which was especially important. If you were dealing with the same criminal across different areas, a uniform investigative procedure that followed tips and leads in a manner to allow comparisons and systematic analysis would have proved particularly beneficial.

In the case of investigating a serial killer, it requires a different approach to those of traditional homicides. In the case of a traditional homicide there's typically some level of connection between the victim and the killer. They are usually connected, or in a relationship or have been involved with each other in a obvious, known way. When it was discovered that showed that victims shared insignificant commonalities, like long hair that was parted between them the process of questioning their relatives had to be honoured. This creates a delay that usually leads to additional murders occurring.

The most notable thing about Bundy's trial was his ability to appear completely different in nearly every image shared to the public or prospective witnesses. For witnesses who saw Bundy around the first of his Seattle-area murders the pictures they were shown did not resemble the person they saw at the exact spot where the victims had disappeared.

When there is a consensus that a serial killer has been active with a plethora of activities that spans several jurisdictions, a multi-agency task force is able to be established. The formation of this task force acknowledges that the agencies are in agreement about how to tackle the issue this is the initial issue to over to allow the efforts of a group to be effective. This helps reduce time spent and puts emphasis on the elements that are crucial to the ultimate goal for the study.

In a serial killing investigation the suspect in question is often among the suspects to be identified at the beginning of. This is what a study of the Bundy investigation confirmed, and will be confirmed in subsequent investigations into serial murder. In the case of Bundy the name of his victim was mentioned three instances by his female friends.

Investigators who were investigating the murders in the Seattle area eventually used their King County payroll computer to aid in the creation of lists of suspects, which narrowed down their hunt for the perpetrator. They contacted the computer to identify common characteristics of the victims. The computer generated four lists including Bundy's and 25 others appearing on each of the four lists. While the data gathered of this computer's primitive modern standards was beneficial however, it is not comparable to the analysis that can be performed by modern technology. Today, computers play a key role in catching serial killers and the fact the databases of databases have been shared, and interconnected via the internet gives a lot of capability to what they accomplish.

Execution

Ted Bundy was put to death by an electric chair on the 24th of January 1989, inside the Florida State prison in the town of Starke at 7:16 am. The deceased was 41 years old. old. age. Outside the prison officers on off duty and death penalty advocates cried out in joy over the news of his death. Bundy is described by his family as "an emotional, tangled mess" in the days before his execution. He spent his last moments in prayer in the presence of an Methodist minister. The minister offered him a final dinner of eggs and steak but he declined. He wept as the prison guards cut off his head and right leg prior to his entry into the prison in which he was to be buried.

It was reported with great fascination it was noted with interest Carol Ann Boone, the former Washington State DES employee who was a friend of Bundy at first as coworkers, on hearing about Bundy's confessions, she decided to walk away from Bundy. She was in such doubt that he could possibly have been the culprit in the crimes he claimed she had stood up for in the past that she packed her belongings and returned to Washington where she was unable to accept his pre-execution telephone call. It was also believed that she was hurt emotionally due to the relationship he had with Diana Weiner, a young Florida attorney. Biographer Ann Rule would later bemoan the fact that many young women felt grief and sadness after the execution of Bundy who was unable to see that the tiny appearance and charm was just an illusion to hide the true monster inside that was unable to feel any other emotion than the desire to control them through taking them down.

Bundy recognized his members of his family, a minister and his lawyer who were sitting outside the chamber, who were able to see through the Plexiglas window and nodded. He smiled at those prosecutors that had found him. Four guards strapped him to the electric chair. He was interrogated by the prison's director to say if he had any last words. "Yes" said he to his attorney and minister, "I'd like you to send my love and affection for my loved ones and my friends." The microphone was removed , and his face was covered in a the dark leather hood. Electrodes were put on his leg that was shaved and his head. The prison's manager was on the phone to determine whether a stay extension was allowed. The phone was empty. He shook his head in recognition of the executioner in hood who turned the switch and sprayed the body of Bundy with 2,000 volts in the early morning hours of 7:06. He died just 10 minutes later.

Chapter 7: Victims' Family Involving

Closure And Sentiments

The first month following her daughter was missing from the parking area of Bountiful and Utah's Viewmont High parking lot, Debi Kent's mother was sleeping on her sofa next to the window that overlooked the street right next to her house. The dream she had was that someone would pass through and drop her missing daughter's body on her front lawn. She would awake and look out into the darkness, but there was nothing. The months turned into years, and after a decade gone by, they purchased burial plots. Three years later, they built the headstone. Then, 14 years after she disappeared, Ted Bundy confessed to murdering and burying her body. The family awoke at dawn on the day of the execution. There was no huge relief, and certainly not celebration. Debi's younger sister was hoping she was going to feel relieved, however, she was left being depressed inside. Debi's mother was sympathetic to Bundy's mom, saying she felt so sad for a woman who was able to raise a child like Bundy and not be able to know.

The the Florida State University's Chi Omega sorority house remembered the specifics of the night of the horrific assaults as if they were yesterday on the day when Bundy was executed. The victims' roommates noted that the entire house had just returned from their holiday break, and everyone was smiling and wishing goodnight to one another. Over the last 11 years, members of sororities and certain victims are in a state of confusion as they attempt to comprehend why they couldn't have heard anything that would have brought them awareness of the suffering of their loved ones dying and allowed them to assist the victims before it was too far too late. A thin wall was all that was separating the victims from those who could have quickly stepped in to help them. The image of those who were victims of the attack falling across the hall or lying bloody and dead in their bed is an unforgettable recollection which is often recalled. The incident was too painful to bear for Valerie Duke, who dropped out of school , and later took her own life. The consequences that lingered throughout the years brought immense hurt and derailment of careers and also anger with emergency and police personnel who were looking for victims rather than immediately taking Lisa Levy to the hospital. The police advised them to stay apart from each other and not to discuss the incident, which caused the victims feeling slighted by the people who should have been coming to help. One member of the sorority praised Bundy's ability to obey laws when she interrogated her during a preliminarily deposition. Bundy could even recall specific details, allowing him to inquire about the place where her trash container was set up, and how it was placed against the door to stop it from being slammed. The sisters believe that it is a travesty to their fellow members of the sorority to be killed in such a horrendous and violent death at the age of just. As Bundy was about to be put to execution, one woman said "I believe tomorrow I'll be messy however, I will go to continue working just like usual. For the family members of his victims and their families, at the end of this long it will be a sense of peace."

Chapter 8: The Arrest Trial And Escape

Success

Bundy was incarcerated on August 16 in 1975, at Salt Lake City, for inability to stop for an officer of the law. The search in his car found a ski mask handcuffs, a crowbar trash bags, an icepick and other items that were believed by the police to be tools for theft. Bundy kept his cool at the moment of questioning, stating that he required the snowboarding mask and that he had discovered the handcuffs in the trash. Utah Investigator Jerry Thompson connected Bundy and his Volkswagen to the DaRonch kidnapping as well as the missing girls. He also checked his apartment.

The search turned up the sales brochure for Colorado ski resorts. The brochure had an entry for an address called the Wildwood Inn where Caryn Campbell disappeared. After inspecting his apartment and a search warrant was issued, authorities took Bundy into a line-up in front of DaRonch and the many witnesses. They identified Bundy to be "Officer of Roseland" and also as the person that was sleeping in his home the night Debby Kent vanished.

After a lengthy trial lasting a week, Bundy was found guilty of kidnapping DaRonch on the 1st of March in 1976. She was sentenced to 15 year at the Utah State Jail. Colorado authorities were investigating murder charges, however the case was dismissed, and Bundy was extradited to Colorado to be tried.

On the 7th of June 1977, as he was preparing for a court hearing for the Caryn Campbell murder trial, Bundy was brought to the Pitkin County court house in Aspen. In the course of a recess in court, the judge allowed him to enter the law library at the courthouse in which he jumped out of the building from the second floor window, and then left but injured his right ankle in the plunge. At the time. after the escape of Bundy, Bundy initially was able to run and then moved slowly through the village until Aspen Mountain.

It was able to make it all the up to the summit the summit of Aspen Mountain without being spotted after which he took a rest for two weeks in an empty cabin. However, in the later days he lost his direction and wandered around the mountain, leaving out two routes that lead down the mountain to his preferred destination, which was that is, Crested Butte. In one instance when he was in the town, he met with a gun-toting citizen who was one of those looking Aspen Mountain for Ted Bundy However, he managed to talk himself away from danger.

On June 13 in 1977 Bundy was driving an old car that he discovered at the top of the mountain. He returned to Aspen and was able to escape however, two cops deputies noticed the car with dim headlights that were weaving through its lane , and took Bundy over. They recognized him and took Bundy back to the prison. Bundy was in jail for six days.

He was detained again and was released, however Bundy was working on a new escape strategy. He was held at prison in the Glenwood Springs, Colorado, prison as he waited for his trial. He was able to obtain the hacksaw blade along with 500 dollars but later stated that the blade was a gift from a prisoner. In two months, he cut through the welds to repair the small metal plate that was in the ceiling. Eventually, after the flames had cooled, he was able to pass through the hole to access the crawl space that was above.

A prisoner informant informed guards that he observed Bundy moving the ceiling around the hour of his nights prior to his escape, however the matter was never investigated. The Bundy's Aspen trial judge declared on December 22nd 1977 for his Caryn Campbell's murder trial was to start on January 9 in 1978, and then moved the trial in Colorado Springs, Bundy realized that he had to plan his escape before being removed from his prison in Glenwood Springs prison.

In the evening of December the 30th of December, 1977 Bundy was warm and cozy and put with books and documents under his blanket in order to appear as if he was asleep. He moved through the hole before climbing upwards in the crawlspace. Bundy moved across to an area over the jailer's linen closetThe jailer as well as his wife were there for the night. was able to get into the condo of the jailer and then walked out the door.

Bundy was not in jail however he was walking amid an icy cold white Colorado night. He was driving a damaged MG and it stopped on the mountain. Bundy was trapped on the side of Interstate 70 in the middle of the night, in an icy storm, but another driver gave him a comfortable journey to Vail. Then he took the bus to Denver and then boarded the TWA at 8:55 a.m. plane to Chicago. It was reported that the Glenwood Springs prison guards didn't notice that Bundy disappeared until twelve at night on December 31 1997, just the 17th hour after his escape at the date Bundy had already arrived in Chicago.

Florida

After his arrival after his arrival in Chicago, Bundy then caught an Amtrak train that took him to Ann Arbor, Michigan, which is where he was able to secure a room within the YMCA. The 2nd of January in 1978 the two of them attended the Ann Arbor bar and watched the University of Washington Huskies, the team from his school beat Michigan during the Rose Bowl. The next day, he drove off in an automobile from Ann Arbor, which he abandoned at Atlanta, Georgia before boarding the bus to Tallahassee, Florida, where the bus arrived on the 8th January 1978. In Tallahassee, he was able to lease an apartment at a boarding house under the name of "Chris Hagen" and was involved in numerous petty criminal actions, such as theft of handbags, shoplifting and vehicle theft. He snatched the student ID card which was from Kenneth Misner and sent out to get documents from misner's Social Security card and birth certificate. He was bald and made a fake mole on his cheek before heading out and, other than this, he did not make any attempt to disguise himself. Bundy looked for work on the construction and building site however, when the construction officer demanded Bundy to show his driver's license to be recognized, Bundy left. That was his sole effort in job search.

After Bundy's arrival in Tallahassee in the early morning hours on Super Bowl Sunday on January 15th, 1978 two and two and a half years of bloodthirsty violence began. Bundy went to the Florida State University Chi Omega sorority residence at about 3 a.m. And killed two asleep ladies, Lisa Levy and Margaret Bowman. Bundy was bludgeoned and strangled Levy and Bowman as well as assaulted sexually Levy. He also bludgeoned the two others Chi Omegas: Karen Chandler and Kathy Kleiner. The entire episode lasted no more than a half-hour. After leaving Chi Omega's Chi Omega home, Bundy moved into a home a few blocks away, and was clubbing there. He also seriously injured Florida State College student Cheryl Thomas.

On the 9th of February of 1978 Bundy set out for Lake City, Florida. There, he abducted murdered, raped and even murdered 12 year old Kimberly Leach, tossing her body in a shed made of pigs. In February in 1978 Bundy got another

Volkswagen Beetle and left Tallahassee for good, driving west through into the Florida panhandle.

On the 15th of February 1978, shortly at one a.m., Bundy was detained by Pensacola policemen David Lee. After the officer performed the check on the plate of registration, the vehicle was found to be stolen. Bundy got into a dispute with the officer until being finally put to death. When Lee led the suspect, who was unidentified, to the prison, Bundy said "I wish I had been killed." In his court appearance, Bundy provided the authorities with an address Ken Misner (and presented taken acknowledgement of Misner) However, police from the Florida Department of Police made an acceptable finger print identification on the same day. He was swiftly moved to Tallahassee and was then was charged with being involved in Tallahassee as well as the Lake City murders. Later, he was taken to Miami to be tried for Chi Omega. Chi Omega killings.

Conviction and execution

Bite mark testimony during The Chi Omega trialBundy went to trial for the Chi Omega murders in the month of June 1979 in the presence of Dade County Circuit Court Judge Edward D. Cowart administering. Despite having five court appointed attorneys, he demanded acting as his own attorney and even cross-examined witnesses. And that included the policeman who discovered Margaret Bowman's corpse. He was charged by the Assistant State Lawyer Larry Simpson.

Two pieces of evidence proved crucial. The first and most important, Chi Omega member Nita Neary, who returned to the home at a very late hour after an evening out she saw Bundy when he left and recognized him when he appeared in the courtroom. Then, in the course of the bloodthirsty trend, Bundy attacked Lisa Levy in her left butt, leaving obvious bite marks. Police obtained plaster casts of her teeth, and forensics experts was able to match them to photos of the Levy's injuries. Bundy is found innocent of all counts and sentenced death. After confirming that sentence Cowart handed him the final decision:

It is a requirement to put you to death by a stream of electrical energy. This will is flowing through your body until you die. Look after yourself, boy. I'm telling you with all my heart; take care of yourself Please. It's a complete disaster for this court to witness the total devastation of humankind as I've witnessed within this room. You're a very intense young man. You could have been an excellent attorney I would've been thrilled to have you work before my eyes, however you took it the other way to as a partner. Look after yourself. I don't feel any sadness for you. I would like you to know that. Again, take care of yourself.

Bundy was a suspect in after the Kimberly Leach murder in the year 1980. He was found guilty of all charges in the main, due to the fibers discovered in his van which matched the clothes worn by Leach and an eyewitness who witnessed Bundy leading Leach away from the school, and being sentenced to execution. When the trial began, Kimberly Leach trial, Bundy got married to former friend Carole Ann Boone in the courtroom as she was being questioned at the bar. After numerous visits to the couple, Bundy and his newly married spouse, Boone brought to life an infant in October, 1982. However, in the year 1986, Boone went back to Washington and never went again to Florida. Her exact location as well as that of her daughter are not known.

As he waited for execution at Starke Jail, Bundy was kept in the cell with another serial murderer Ottis Toole, who was the murderer of Adam Walsh. FBI profiler Robert K. Ressler met Bundy in the prison as part of his job speaking to serial killers however, he discovered Bundy insensitive and manipulative, and able to speak in only the 3rd person and only in the abstract. In a 1992 article, Ressler mentioned his impression of Bundy as opposed to his opinions of other serial murderers: "This guy was an animal, and it amazed me to see that media was in a state of confusion."

However during the same time period, Bundy was typically checked out by Unique Representative William Hagmaier of the

Federal Bureau of Investigation's Behavioral Science System. Bundy was able to confide to Hagmaier and even go so far as to call him a friend. In the end, Bundy admitted to Hagmaier numerous details of the murders that were unknown or not officially reported.

In the month of October 1984 Bundy reached out to former King County murder investigator Bob Keppel and offered to assist in the ongoing hunt at The Green River Killer by supplying his own thoughts and analyses. Keppel as well as Green River Job Force investigator Dave Reichert went to Florida's death row to speak to Bundy. The two investigators later said the interviews provided no actual assistance in the investigation. They gave a greater understanding of Bundy's inner thoughts, however they were mostly sought after with the intention of gaining information about the details of murders that were not solved. Bundy was believed to have committed.

Bundy photo of his mugshot, taken in 1980, following his sentence to death for the murder of Kimberly LeachBundy called

Keppel again in 1988. In that time the appeals were exhausted. Bundy was able to defeat death warrants from March 4 in 1986 and July 2nd and November 18th of the year 1986. In the midst of execution, Bundy admitted to 8 major murders that were unsolved that occurred in Washington State for which he was the primary suspect. Bundy admitted to Keppel it was five bodies in Taylor Mountain, not 4 as they initially thought. Bundy acknowledged in detail the murder of Georgeann Hawkins, defining how he lured her to his car, slapped her with a tire iron was stored under his vehicle, and then tried to fend off her in the car with him, and then raped and choked her.

Following an interview Keppel stated that he was stunned when he spoke to Bundy and it was clear that he was a kind of man "born to murder." Keppel mentioned:

He described the Issaquah crime location (where Janice Ott, Denise Naslund along with Georgeann Hawkins had been left) and it seemed as if he were there. It was as if he could see everything. He was in awe due to the fact that he had spent all day there. He's totally obsessed with murder every day.

Bundy believed he would be able to use the information and confessions in part to obtain another stay of execution , or perhaps reduce the sentence to remain in imprisonment time. In one instance an attorney who was employed by Bundy demanded a number family members victims to send letters to Florida Governor Robert Martinez and request for mercy to allow Bundy to find out which graves their beloved loved ones lay. The majority of families declined. Keppel and other witnesses have reported that Bundy did not provide any details about his criminal lapses when he made his confessions. He also promised to reveal more and other body dump sites if was granted "more period of time." This tactic was not successful however and Bundy was executed according to schedule.

The night prior to when Bundy was executed the following night, he appeared on a television talk show interview to James Dobson, head of the evangelical Christian firm Fixate on the Family. In an interview Bundy was repeatedly claiming about the"x-rated "roots" to his criminal actions. He claimed that, even though porn did not cause the murderer however, the use of porn that was violent contributed to "shape and mould" his violent behavior into "conduct which is so horrific that it's impossible to define." He said he was of the opinion that media violence, "specifically sexualized violence," led boys "down the road to becoming Ted Bundys." In the the same conversation, Bundy specified:

" You're going to end my life and it will protect my civilization from me. There are numerous users of porn, and you're not doing anything about it."

According to Hagmaier Bundy considered suicide in the weeks before the execution but decided against it.

at 7:06 a.m. local time on January 24 1989 Ted Bundy was executed in the electric chair at Florida State Jail located in Starke, Florida. His final words were "I would like to show my love to my family, friends as well as my family." Then more than 2 000 volts of electricity were emitted across his body for just two minutes. Bundy was declared deceased at around 7:16 a.m. Around 100 people waiting outside the jail and cheered after they heard the announcement that Bundy had been declared dead.

Victim profiles and Modus operandi

He would try to approach a potential victim in public places at any time, whether in the daytime or with crowds, such as when he abducted Ott as well as Naslund in Lake Sammamish or when he kidnapped Leach at her college. Bundy used a variety of strategies for getting the trust of a victim. In certain instances the perpetrator would attempt to feign injuries, putting the arm while slinging it, or wearing a fake cast, such as the killings of Hawkins and Rancourt, Ott, Naslund, and Cunningham. In other instances, Bundy pretend to be a authority persona; he posed to be a policeman when confronting Carol DaRonch. On the day prior to his murder, Kimberly Leach, Bundy approached another young Florida girl claiming as "Richard Burton from the Fire

Department", however, he left the scene shortly after her brother came up.

Bundy was a unique talent because his facial features were appealing, but not particularly memorable. Later on Bundy was often called chameleon-like. He was capable of looking completely different with only minor changes of his face, e.g., growing beard or changing hairstyle.

The majority of Bundy's victims were white women , and the majority were middle-class. The majority of victims were between 15 and 25 years old. The majority of them were students at universities. in her autobiography, Rule states that the vast majority the victims of Bundy's murders were bald with long straight hair that was split in the middleas in Stephanie Brooks, the woman with whom Bundy was engaged in 1973. Rule suggests that Bundy's bitterness towards his first love was a motivating factor in his murder spree. However, in an interview in 1980, Bundy dismissed this hypothesis:" hey ... you just meet the criteria of being attractive and young ... The truth is that number of people have believed this idea that all the girls had similar hairhaving hair that was the same color and parted at between ... however, when you examine it closely, every single thing was distinct ... in physical appearance the girls were all different."

After dragging a victim towards their vehicle Bundy was able to hit the victim head on using a crowbar that he placed beneath his Volkswagen or concealed within the vehicle. Every skull recovered, except than that of Kimberly Leach, revealed signs of trauma caused by blunt force. Every recovered body apart from the one of Kimberly Leach was able to show evidence of strangulation.

Many of the victims of Bundy's were moved to a considerable distance from the place they went missing, like the case with Kathy Parks, whom he drove over 220 miles Oregon from Oregon to Washington. Bundy usually would consume alcohol prior to locating the victim. Carol DaRonch admitted to smelling alcohol in his breath.

Hagmaier stated that Bundy believed himself to be an uninvolved killer in his early years and then moved to what he believed to be the "prime" as well as his "predator" phase. Bundy stated that his "predator" stage began at the time that he was involved in his involvement in the Lynda Healy murder. This was at which point he began looking for victims he believed to be of equal capability as a killer.

On the death row, Bundy admitted to killing at at least one dozen of his victims using hacksaws. The heads that were severed remained that were later found in Taylor Mountain in his room or at his apartment or condo for a few days before finally disposing of the bodies. He confessed to burning Donna Manson's skull in his flames that he shared with his love. The skulls of the victims of Bundy were discovered with front teeth smashed out. Bundy admitted that he visited the bodies of his victims over and over in his Taylor Mountain body dump site. He admitted that he would lay in their bodies for hours, applying makeup to their bodies , and then making the most of their bodies until putrefaction forced him to leave the body. In the days after his passing, Bundy confessed to going back to the body of Georgeann Hawkins for purposes of necrophilia.

Bundy confessed to having other memorabilia of his crimes. Bundy admitted to keeping other relics of his crimes. Utah authorities who visited at the Bundy's home in 1975 were unable to find a cache of photos that Bundy kept in the energy room. These were pictures that Bundy damaged after returning home following his release under bail. His beloved Elizabeth discovered a suitcase in his room that contained women's clothing.

When Bundy was confronted by police officers who claimed they believed that the total number of persons he committed murder was just 36 Bundy said that police officers should "add one number to that, and you'll have it." Rule speculated that this means Bundy might have killed more than 100 women. Speaking to his attorney Polly Nelson in the year 1988, however, Bundy dismissed the 100plus victims' theory and claimed that the most common estimation of around 35 victims was accurate.

Pathology

On December 27, 1987 Bundy received an analysis for seven hour in a 7-hour session by Dorothy Otnow Lewis, a teacher at New York University Medical Center. Lewis observed Bundy being a manic depression who's criminal activities generally occurred during his depression episodes. For Lewis, Bundy defined his young age, particularly his connection to his grandparents from the past, Samuel and Eleanor Cowell.

According to Bundy the grandpa of his Samuel Cowell was a deacon in his church. Along with the well-established description of his grandfather as a bully who swore to silence, Bundy defined him as racist and a snob who hated people of color, Italians, Catholics, and Jews. He also mentioned that his grandfather was a cruel animal lover including beating the pet of the family dog, and dragging the community cats with his tails. He also shared with Lewis the story of how his grandpa had an extensive collection of porn inside his greenhouse the family, Bundy and a cousin would sneak in to stare at the collection for long periods of time.

The family members expressed doubts about Louise's "Jack Worthington" story of Bundy's family and noted it was true that Samuel Cowell once flew into anger when the subject of the boy's father came up. Bundy identified his grandma as a quiet and loyal companion, who was occasionally taken to hospitals for shock therapy for depression. Near the final stages of her life, Bundy stated that she became agoraphobic.

Louise Bundy's younger sister Julia was able to recall a traumatic event along with her son. After having a rest at the Cowells at home for a nap Julia was awakened to be being surrounded by knives in the Cowell kitchen. Three-year-old Ted was in the bed waiting and was smiling at her.

Bundy used credit cards to buy more than 30 pairs of socks while on the move in Florida He was self-described as a fan of feet.

The Dobson interview prior to the sentence, Bundy said that violent porn was a key factor in his sexual criminal activities. According to Bundy that as a teenager, he was able to find "outside the home once more in the supermarkets of the region or in a local drug store, pornographic material that was referred to as "soft or core ... Also, occasionally, we would come across adult-oriented books with a more complex kind ..."

Bundy declared, "It occurred in phases that grew slowly. What I've experienced with porn in general however, with porn that is violent level of sexuality, it is the moment you are dependent on it and I view this as a type of dependency , like other kinds of dependence--I am always looking for more potent and specific or graphic versions of content. Once you've reached a level that the porn is only assuming it is a jump-off point, where you begin to think whether actually doing it will bring you something that is beyond just having a look."

In a note he wrote quickly before his release from Glenwood Springs prison, Bundy stated "I have met individuals whom ... show vulnerability. Their expressions tell you "I'm afraid of you.' They are tolerant of the abuse ... Because they are expecting to suffer, do they secretly encourage it?"

In a interview from 1980 discussing the validation given to serial killers of his deeds, Bundy said "So what is one less? Which is one less person in the earth?" When Florida investigators requested Bundy to provide the location the place he'd taken Kimberly Leach's body in search of her family's comfort, Bundy apparently said, "But I'm the coldest child of a tinker you'll ever encounter."

Chapter 9: Depths Of Wickedness

While there have been at least 57 documented instances of serial killings in America in the years prior to 1900, Bundy changed the landscape. The man who admitted to killing at thirty women in the period between 1973 and 1978and some experts think Bundy killed more than a hundred -- was an outstanding bad guy in a number of ways.

" In 1974, when we first had our first criminal act that we knew of, the crime wasn't well-known," said Robert Keppel an earlier murder investigator and the author of The Riverman which recounts his hunt to find the Washington's Green River Killer and his efforts to get Ted Bundy's help. "What sets him apart over the rest is the variety of his crimes and the time frame in which he carried out murders that crossed state lines, and across the entire country," Keppel said. Bundy killed up to 10 states, which is greater than the number of serial murderers during American history.

University of Louisville criminology professor Ronald M. Holmes, who was a referee for two years Bundy and questioned the killer in prison the tendency of Bundy to travel was a result of the development of the nation's interstate system and the increasing reliability of transportation. Prior to Bundy the majority of serial killers were killed in their own backyards.

Bundy was among the first person to depart from this pattern, and he created the model that is used today by many killers. A brand new kind of killer Bundy was a new kind of criminal that authorities had never previously encountered. They were still not prepared to deal with his case. "His incident had a significant impact as police gathered information about murderers," Keppel said. "There was no central repository for information on murders in the US in the early days."

Though some experts do not agree, Keppel said the Bundy incident was a major factor in the creation of VICAP (Violent Criminal Apprehension Program) VICAP, an FBI database that was created to collect information on serial murders. The FBI began using VICAP in 1985.

Bundy's geographic variety made detectives tired of the task of contacting individual authorities departments throughout the U.S.A. and combing through the many murder files. It was Bundy as a proxy who provided the FBI how important it was to have an overall database of murders. "It took me and me a year to compile information on over 90 murders across Western state," said Keppel. "If everyone had cooperated as part of VICAP, and everyone cooperated in the VICAP program and had reported their criminal acts and it was referred to the VICAP program, it could have been referred in only a few seconds."

The most talked about media star - Bundy and a little help of the press, altered the appearance of serial murderers, too. According to Holmes who has profiled more than 350 murder and rape cases the public perception that the serial murderer had prior to Bundy was that of a psychotic crazy berserk with physical issues.

" Then Bundy appears and says, 'Hey! I'm like the man next door. I'm the completely stranger right next to you''" Holmes said, describing the title of the criminal offense Author Ann Rule's work on Bundy. Holmes claimed that the serial killers prior to Bundy who were equally charming as they were American, but weren't able to get the fame Bundy had. "We serial killers have become your children, we're your spouses and we're everywhere," Bundy is quoted in Harold Schechter's novel, The A to Z Encyclopedia of Serial Killers. The author holds a Ph.D. on serial murder, Bundy utilized a range of serial killer traits and had a vast amount of insanity. According to multiple reports, he had headless heads at house, and was a lonely man who was also engaged to two women as killing.

He burned skulls inside his fireplace and removed the cremated remains. He dressed dead victims in new clothes as well as ate their flesh. faked lameness to draw the attention of victims and created fake accents. The victim remained for nine days. He was twice removed from custody. He was a master cat burglar and demanded the strangulation of his victims as he stared at them straight in the eyes.

Bundy thought of serial killing as an unsettling mixture of sport, craft as well as intellectual endeavor. An investigation report from 1992 revealed that Bundy was known to go on off-road run, "getting a woman and then releasing her, unharmed, to test his skills." In his interviews, he described killing with learning to become a more skilled cook or technician. He claimed to recruiters that he had the distinction of having a Ph.D. for serial murder. Only the most effective victims were eliminated The most significant influence on public's awareness was the scope of his crime and the identity of the victims. Bundy didn't murder sexual workers or drug dealers. He killed the police chief's daughter. He murdered pretty college girls. His crimes sparked outrage and prompted across the nation media coverage. "He killed the most beautiful and most attractive of the young people," said Holmes. "He was murdering college girls who represented considered to be the next generation of America. They were very crucial victims."

As his own counsel, Bundy dragged out his execution for nearly 11 years. The telecasts of his trial in Miami was broadcast into homes in the evening news. At the time of his executed in 1989, at the age of 42 years old, Bundy became so widely disliked that, as per Schechter's autobiography there were crowds of people outside the prison where he was set to be electrocuted , to celebrate his demise with champagne. All across the states of Washington, Keppel said pubs in every city had signs to commemorate his execution "Drink one for Bundy."

Ted Bundy Quotations

Ted Bundy is attempting to explain something to you. Be attentive to what he has to say:

" It's not a straightforward thing to differentiate things. It's about events that may in themselves create tension or pressure, could or be undesirable in one way or the other, or exert an unsettling effect. It is important to consider the impact of each event in the context of its particular effect on the particular person. There are no generalizations or predictions you could make. You can't anticipate behavior similar to this. While society would like to believe that it can identify bad people but however, if someone is seen to be doing something that's unsocial and dangerous, it's an indication of something else that's happening within them. When they are doing something that is deviant, they are detected. Forecasts can't be made until the point at which they occur."

" I believe it is possible to affirm that the effect on the individual's family background was positive. However, it was not enough positive-- not long-lasting and perhaps not enough to ward off the desires or compulsions that caused this incident and the effects of the family and environment where this person was raised were positive, however, they were not enough to the person in question" "You decide to take the person you're discussing and then subject him to stress. Tension can occur arbitrarily however its effect on the character isn't random. it identifies. This causes a certain amount of chaos, confusion and even disappointment. The person begins looking at a possible target for his displeasures. The continual nature of this stress this person was experiencing-- the character of the flaw or defect of his persona, along with other elements in the world that provide him with a suitable opportunity to blame his failures on or aversion to realityresults in the situation that we're discussing. There's no trigger, but it's much more complex than the previous."

" I am not a fan of using the terms mental or psychiatric because there aren't any stereotypes and once you start to apply these labels, you cease to take seriously details." "This situation isn't immediately recognized by the individual or considered as a major issue. It is a kind of manifestation through an interest in sexual behavior, such as sexual pictures . But this curiosity is, for an unidentified reason will eventually be geared to issues related to sexuality that include violence. I cannot stress enough the constant progress of this. It's not just a temporary thing. in a totally different way that this individual would deal with women on a daily basis but not in the context of sexual health, because there's a place over here such as collecting stamps. He doesn't keep the taste of glue in a sense, throughout the day long. In a more expansive abstraction it begins to occupy him."

" He doesn't have any hatred towards women. There's no evidence in his past that could suggest that there was abuse from women. There's a certain kind of weakness that causes this individual's desire for the kind of sexual sex, including violence that will slowly begin to take over some of his dreams. He was not thinking about performing these actions however he did get pleasure by watching others who were who were so involved. The end result would be that the passion could become such a demand for new information that it would be addressed through what he could discover in unclean book stores."

" Imagine you were walking down the street at night and then, completely, when he happened to look up at the window of a house where he saw an elderly woman dressed in her underwear. Then he began with a certain consistency, and with greater consistency to canvass, in a way the area he was living in. Through looking through windows, like, watching women get dressed, or watching anything that was on the screen at the hour of night and approaching it as a job, throwing himself into it for a long time.

When he was a teenager, he would go around the communities who were a part of his, and look for locations in which he could view the things he desired to see in general, these occasions were decided by the person's normal life. Therefore, he wouldn't delay or put off an important, significant event. He did not change his schedule to accommodate this excessive voyeuristic behavior. The man gained a lot of satisfaction from this. In the end, he was highly proficient at itlike anyone who can become proficient at doing anything that they can do repeatedly. What began to happen was that issues weren't being disrupted or reorganized due to this behavior, but , as time went on the events were delayed or changed to work around long hours in the streets, during the evening, as well as during the morning hours."

" What's happening is that we're developing the disorder and what could have been a predisposition to violence end becoming an individual. As the condition progresses and its goals or features become more precisely defined the condition begins to demand more attention from the individual. There's a specific degree of stress, or struggle between the typical person and psychopathological entity. The tension between the normal person as well as the normal awareness of the person and the needs that are that are being imposed upon him through this battling the condition within him seems to be battling for more attention . And it's not an isolated issue. The one isn't turned on , and the other does not switch off. They're both active in different ways simultaneously. In certain situations there is a difference in which one may be the more energetic."

" A point could be reached when we'd have all this that tank of stress structure.

Structure and building. In the end, it is certain that this force- this entity would bring about an improvement. It might not be significant but a substantial advancement could be madewhere the pressure could be excessive and the demands as well as expectations for this organization would grow to the point that they cannot be managed. This is where the consequences could be clearly seen in the very first instance."" I believe that you could get a bit more sense of this by considering the effects of alcohol. It is crucial to consider that when someone drank cheaply the inhibitions of his were greatly diminished. The desire to take part in voyeuristic behavior on trips to the book store was greater, more frequent, and more urgent. Each time the participant was involved in this type of conduct the man was drunk."

" In one particular evening, after he'd consumed a lot and was walking past the bar, he saw an individual leave the bar and walking up an unlit side street. We'd like to say that there was no desire to help the person he saw took him-in a way that the man had never had before. It was a very intense experience for him. It got to the point that the moment he did not give a amount in thought, he scoured around for an instrument that he could take on this woman. He found the two-by-four somewhere and continued to track and follow the woman until he came to the point that the urge to do something. there was absolutely no way to control in this particular moment. The kind of experience that was discovered and the ferocious need to do it into the unknown, which actually brought an entirely new dimension to the portion of him who was bewildered by violent acts, sexual sex and women-- a mix of thing. The definition is not particularly clear however, it became more clear as time passed."

" On nights of prosperity, he began to move around this identical area, enthralled by the image he'd observed on the night before and one particular time the woman he observed parking her car and then walk up to her front door. She was fumbling in her deeds. He followed her and hit her with an object of wood was on his person. She fell and began screaming, and he screamed and fled. The actions he took been a complete frightening for him. The repercussions of this was to some time, to close the fractures. and to avoid doing any activity. The first time, he was relaxed and declared to himself that he wouldn't repeat that mistake or anything that could lead to it. He did every thing he was supposed to do. He was cautious and didn't go out at night. While he was drinking alcohol, he was surrounded by with his friends. Over the course of a few months, the repercussions of his actions remained to him. He observed his behavior and grew the desire to tackle the things he began to see as a few things that were more severe than he believed they were. within a short time the impact of this incident was no longer deterrent. In the following months, afterward, he began looking through windows and falling back into his old routine. When the repulsion began to diminish some thing stuck to him. This was the risk that was so terrifying that he took by allowing him to engage in sudden, unintentional violent acts. It took six months or sobefore he was returned to thinking of alternative ways of participating in similar activities, but nothing which is likely to trigger fear."

" Another night when he saw a woman walk to her home, he followed her. In the end, he came up with the plan to attack her inside the early hours of the morning, he entered her bedroom, got into the bed of the woman and tried to control the extent of her ... the only thing that he was able to accomplish was waking her up and causing her to panic and shout. He was quickly out of the room. the next day, he was met by the same kind of repulsion, disgust and doubt what prompted him to engage in such brutal violence. But the point was that he had done exactly the same thing as the previous time, he was away from the streets, vowed to never repeat it, and acknowledged the horrifying things he'd committed, and certainly was shocked by what he witnessed taking place, it took him only 3 months to overcome the incident, and following the second incident was over in just a month until it took any time at all to recover ... "

" It's about abstracted, confidential living and breathing persons however they weren't known. At times, they were signs, but once an exact point of the relationship was crossed, they became individuals and became in fact, problems, but that's not the same word ... this is when the rational self-- the normal selfwould come out and respond with horror and fear. However, the typical self accepting the current circumstances, the typical self would conspire with this other aspect of him to cover up the crime. The survival trumped regret in the typical person, and began to change psychologically, with no guilt using a variety of methods. The idea that it was normal, it was acceptable and needed and it went on and on."

" He didn't get any satisfaction from inflicting damage or causing hurt to the person whom he attacked. He definitely did not feel satisfaction from causing pain. He tried everything in the right way, while contemplating the absurdity of the situationand not to harm those people at the very minimum but not in a physical way."

The following are statements made by Ted about the kidnapping as well as the murder of a college co-ed aged 21 Lynda Healy. It happened on the 31st of January 1974. Healy was taken from the basement bedroom of her home, where she was shown others students. It was more than a year prior to her decomposing remains being discovered and so were the remains of three other girls lying on the slopes in Taylor Mountain.

" He looked at the house and discovered that front doors were unlocked. He thought about the possibility of opening it. What was the chance it provided, and returned to the house later and entered the house. Then he went through the house, and found one door, which he then openedit up. He was truly lucky to missed and hit. I don't know the reason, or who it was, and not looking for anyone who could possibly provide the best chance. It was late in the night. Most likely, everyone would be asleep . But we do are aware that some time later , the remains were discovered somewhere inside the Cascades. It is probable that she travelled to a place that was quiet and private. His house or an unreachable location. He'd have her dress in a new outfit and after that, with this part of him happy and content, he was in a situation where the moment came when he realized there was no way to let her go. At that point, she would be killed and then leave her body in the place the body was."

" In terms of regret about the incident can be felt, it will be for a period of time. But, it may be justified. Someone might try to prove the claim by saying "Well I'm sorry, it was your fault this time however, you're never going to repeat it. Therefore, let's all remain together and this will never occur again." Why should this person be sacrificed for the rest of his life? But this didn't last lengthy. It took a few weeks. We begin to enter semi-dormancy and then it would re-invigorate itself, in one way or another. When the condition started to assert its power and it didn't look back. It looked ahead. I didn't want to dwell about the past however, it was time to begin planning and anticipate, think about the next lessons to be discovered. Experience is a teacher in both obvious as well as subtle methods.

Over a period of time it would be easier to avoid anxiety and less confusion, and there would be less fear and anxiety. It would be a more rapid regrowth."

What We Can Learn from Ted Bundy

He was a former deputy director for his Seattle Criminal offense Avoidance advisory committee. He also wrote an e-book to advise women to avoid rape. One-time Boy Scout with an appealing career with respect to Washington political circles, Ted Bundy seemed an excellent example of a decent and a decent citizen. But, beneath the hospitable exterior, there was a force that put him in an electric chair during the month of Jan of this year.

In the final hours prior to his popular execution for the murder of up to 50 girls and women of Utah, Washington, Idaho, Colorado and Florida, the serial killer sought Christian psychotherapist James Dobson to visit him in his home in the Florida State Jail. Bundy had recommended Doc. Dobson as a former member of the President Reagan's Commission on Porn - for two years prior to their meeting. While a throng of journalists stood on the outside Bundy talked to Dobson about the consequences of porn for his behaviour.

Bundy stated that he began reading pornography at 13 or 12 years old. age. Some of his friends discovered books with X-rated ratings in the garbage bins in the community: "From time to time we would find adult books that were more difficult in nature and a more graphic, particular kind of book than what we see at the local grocery store," he told Dobson in the interview taped. "But slowly over time, reading porn began to end becoming a deadly habit. "My experience with porn is that when you are hooked, (and I look at this as a form of dependency, similar to other kinds of dependence) I'd continue seeking out more powerful or more specific, visually appealing forms of content. As with a dependency, you constantly seek something more challenging to resist, something that will give you a greater feeling of satisfaction. When you get to a point where the porn's only assuming you're at that jumping off point at which you begin to think about whether you could actually do it to bring you something more than just reading about or taking a glance at the subject."

After a few years, the sexually induced desires were manifested in the first time he committed a murder. Although Bundy claimed he was not a victim of porn, he said that adult material influenced and shaped his actions. He also warned the nation that "the most dangerous forms of porn contain sexual violence and violence. The wedding of these two forces, which I've experienced well, reveals the hatred that's impossible to describe."

Bundy claimed his porn "nabbed me from my house 20-30 years ago and today porn is able to be a link and pull a child out of any place." Morality and his spiritual training at first prevented him from pursuing his desires however, he confessed that eventually, "I could not keep behind any longer." Alcohol was said to have broken the restrictions that led him to commit his first crime. "What alcohol did with exposure to porn reduced my inhibitions at the same time, the ideal life that was fueled by porn further weakened them."

In the course of the murders, Bundy claimed the feeling was that he was being controlled by "something terrible and alien. There's no way to describe the initial need to do this sort of thing. After the fact that it's been satisfied or not and decreases, you can be able to say, or even spend the energy level decreases and I generally become me again." "However generally I was a normal person. I wasn't some man who went to bars or being a bottom. I wasn't an alcoholic in the sense of people who glance at people and say, 'I believe there's something wrong it's easy to discern.' I was a normal person," Bundy told Dobson. "The basic human being and the spirit of fundamentality that God has given me were unharmed however, I regrettably ended up becoming overwhelmed from time to time."

Ted Bundy acknowledged that he was deserving of the death penalty even however, there were anti-death-charge protesters outside his prison cell right up to the time that he was executed. "I ought to be given the harshest penalty that humanity has," he said. "But I don't want to die. I'm kidding you." Dobson claimed that Bundy was crying several times during the conversation "He expressed great regret regret over what did he do, and for the families who suffered." Bundy spent his final night praying with a pastor who was from Gainesville, Florida.

Bundy's final remarks of apology and warning against porn are echoes of statistics, research and studies conducted during the last decade on the relationship between sexual violence and porn criminal acts. Unfortunately, many of the advice in these reports remain unobserved and porn is dismissed as an essential crime.

Based on a study conducted by a team comprising psychologists Neil Malamuth of UCLA, Gene Abel of Columbia University as well as William Marshall of Kingston Penitentiary Different types of porn could trigger thoughts that can lead to criminal activities. In a study of 18 rapists who used "consenting" porn to trigger a sexual assault seven of them claimed that it was a clue to induce the desire to have sex with a force.

A study published by University of New Hampshire has found that the states that have the highest readership of porn magazines such as Playboy as well as Penthouse as well have highest rate of rape. According to the Michigan State Authorities department realized that porn was employed or replicated for 41 percent of sexual assaults they have looked at.

It was found that the Free Congress Research Study and Education Structure discovered that half of criminals who were studied had used porn that was soft to excite themselves before seeking out an accomplice. While media experts and researchers could speculate on the impact of pornography, they claim that it is a that it's a defense under the freedom of speech provisions of the Constitution is a good thing - implementing proof seems to be more akin to a nationwide investigation into pornography as a necessary tool to deter criminals from committing crimes.

In the past few years as more of this type of research has been published significant gains have seen against pornographers, as major retailers have taken care to rid themselves of pornography off their shelves. Ted Bundy's confessions made to Dr. James Dobson - a leader of the largest sector of pro-family organizations across the United States - guarantees to support the initiatives being taken at local and state levels to end porn issues.

Chapter 10: The Birth Of Killer

The boy who would later be Ted Bundy was born on November 24, 1946 in the idyllic village located in Burlington, Vermont. It was his birth name Theodore Robert Cowell. Cowell was not born into the most hospitable of homes or even a house in any way. He was born at the Elizabeth Lund Home for Unwed Mothers, which was a kind of refuge for women who found themselves unmarried and in the time that being in this state could mean they were removed from their homes by their families. The mother of Ted was Eleanor Louise Cowell, known by the most common name of Louise. She was 22 years old older at the time Ted became a baby. The paternity of Ted has, however, for a long time been in doubt.

On the birth certificate of Theodore Cowell The birth certificate mentions that Lloyd Marshall was given as the name of his father, who was a local salesman, and a an air force veteran from his World War Two air force. There was no relationship with Ted and Lloyd and his mother Louise would later alter the facts about Ted's paternity. In some instances she would provide his father's name as Jack Worthington, a sailor whom she claimed she was "seduced" with. A fatherless family in any form could be detrimental to Ted. FBI studies have revealed that 43 percent of serial killers were without the support of one parent. However, there's a more sinister theory concerning Ted Bundy's paternity which transcends the rumors of absenteeism and lies.

Family members of Ted's were long-time believers and the notion is now part of Bundy folklore that Ted was fathered by his grandfather during an incestuous, sexually sexy act with his daughter. According to what we have learned about Louise's dad, it could not be out of his nature. There are several stories about how he discovered the truth about his birth. He once told his girlfriend that one of his cousins in a fit of bullying in a juvenile way, been able to call Ted an "bastard" and presented him with the birth certificate to prove it. Biographers of his claimed that he found it himself. Another account claims that Ted didn't discover the truth for many years, and only after the time he reached adulthood. Whatever method he used to discover about the facts, Ted carried with him the feeling of anger toward his mother who was hiding the truth from him and refusing to speak the truth.

Following Ted's first birth Ted had to be left behind in Vermont with family members while his mother moved to her home town of Philadelphia. They remained for three months separated, but finally Louise took care of Ted and the two were able to move into the home of Louise's parents. They stayed for three years together with Samuel as well as Eleanor Cowell. The Cowells did not raised as a grandchild. Samuel Cowell adopted baby Ted in hopes that he would not be accused of having a birth outside of the marriage. In the end, Ted was presented to the world as a brand new Cowell child, a little sibling to Louise. When he was a child, that was the only thing Ted was aware of. When he learned of the fact that Ted's "parents" weren't actually their grandparents Ted Bundy showed little displeasure towards them when talking about his early years. Based on his own account, Eleanor Cowell was a timid woman who did as her husband told her to do, an insecure woman who sought electroconvulsive therapy for depression. If the accounts of her husband are accurate the obedience of her husband and depression are explicable.

Based on the accounts of both sides of within and without the Cowell Family, Samuel Cowell was not an ideal parent. Samuel was a racist who was a snob against blacks, Irish, Italians, and Jews. Samuel was an atypical schizophrenic and was able to communicate with invisible people. He was a savage to those surrounding him, beating his dog and wife in equal amounts. He was often angry particularly when Ted's paternity even spoken of. He was known to throw his neighbors over his fence with a tail after it had walked into his yard numerous times. One time, he threw his youngest child Julia down a flight of stairs because she had slept too much. In spite of all this, Ted looked up to Samuel and began to recognize Samuel.

The chaos that surrounded the Cowell household was already impacting the young Ted. He began to show an fascination with the macabre, and particularly death. His aunt or, in his mind at the time, his "sister," Julia said she woke up with her bed covered with knives. The knives surrounded her, and were just inches away off her face. When she raised her head to gaze at the bottom on her mattress, she could see Ted sitting on the bed with a huge smile on his tiny face.

Ted's life took a turn for the better in 1950 when his mother changed her name from Nelson and made the decision to move west in order to be with her family. It was in Tacoma, Washington, that Louise got to know John Bundy at a church meeting. In 1951, they were married, and John adopted young Ted who at first, was known by the name he became famous for. In the year 1951, six-year old Ted was developing a new peculiarity in his personality. He was obsessed with material wealth and materialism. The boy was frightened to no end over the amount of income his new stepfather had during his time in the military. Ted was even embarrassed by the thought of someone from his family driving an automobile that was "sensible" such as the Rambler. He would even take his mother through town, having her gaze at the windows of the most expensive retail stores in Philadelphia.

Ted was in a complicated relationship with both his parents. Ted and John weren't close as Ted insisting on using his stepfather's first name rather than any kind of family name. Although John was always trying to invite Ted in family gatherings, Ted always complained about being left out by a man whom described as "not particularly smart." Ted also made the effort not to meet anyone of the four siblings he shared. Ted and Louise On contrary were extremely close. They were both confused about their relationship while when he was a child, and would refer to Louise as his mother and sister. In spite of the bitterness Ted had for her mother, she was able to defend Ted throughout the time she was alive. After Ted's confession and trial, and ultimately conviction, Ted's mother has did not stop defending Ted as a man who was innocent.

Despite Ted's complicated reactions towards his parents his departure from the Cowell household was peaceful and free of any abuse.

Portrait of The Killer A Young Man

When he was a young man, Ted was described very positively by his peers. They described him as a happy and bright childwho was very social and well-liked by his friends and in good academic standing. However, when Ted reached puberty, the boy began to display really odd behaviors.

When he was in Tacoma, Ted recalls doing various odd things in town, most of them due to a teen obsession with women and an ever-growing sexual voyeuristic tendencies. He would walk around the city at night, digging through dumpsters and trash bins hoping to find naked images of women. In these pursuits He also collected crime novel detective magazines, particularly those that reported the instances of sexual assault. He also had a particular fascination with magazines that featured graphic images of injured or killed victims. In the evenings, he would get drunk and stroll around the neighborhood looking for windows that were not covered, that let him see women dressed in a state of unrequited.

In high school Ted admitted to himself that Ted was not a social butterfly and was a bit shy. Although he was still recognized at school, and was classified by fellow students as being a "medium size fish in a huge pond" it was not well-known as he could have been when his younger years. The grades of his students were impacted. He became increasingly insecure as the number of nights he spent in bed increased and he became tongue-tied when in social settings. The anxiety he felt was not only limited to women but also to anyone new that he came across. His primary activity was skiing, and was practiced by using stolen equipment. When he was in his senior year of High School, Ted had been arrested for auto theft and burglary and was gaining an image as something of an oddball. Ted's psyche was a complex one and continued to haunt him during his college years.

The year 1965 was the time that Ted Bundy started college at the University of Puget

Sound before moving within the same year at The University of Washington in Seattle. His field of study was Chinese. In China, Ted discovered his first lover with a fellow student known as Stephanie Brooks. She was beautiful young lady who wore her dark hair in a long bob and split in the middle. In the past, Ted was content.

In 1968 Ted became dissatisfied in his college experience and decided to drop out. He began to bounce from the minimum wage to the minimum wage employment. He also took his first attempt at politics by working at the local office of Nelson Rockefeller and also attending his first Republican National Convention as a delegate for Rockefeller. At this point, Stephanie had become fed over Ted's stagnant career path. She left Ted at the end of the year and returned back in California but leaving Ted grieving. The only thing that was good in the life of the teenager was that it had gone into the ground, and he made the decision to move out of Washington and begin a journey through the nation. He decided to go towards the east of Philadelphia to visit his family and stop for a while in Arkansas in addition to Colorado.

In Philly the city, Ted attended one term during his time at Temple University and, according to some reports, could have finally discovered that he was not his parents. However, by the fall of 1969 Ted returned to Washington where he was able to meet divorcée Elizabeth Kloepfer (who Bundy has used as a name like Meg Anders, Beth Archer as well as Liz Kendall) with whom the couple would have a volatile relationship that was sporadic for a long time. However, for the time being, Ted seems to have stabilized thanks to Liz along with his own mother who was there for Ted even when he had young children that he had to care for.

In the year 1970, Ted started to turn his life around. He enrolled again at UW as majoring in psychology, where he was on the honor roll and was a beloved of several Professors. The year was 1971. He was a member of the local suicide hotline, and made friends with an ex-police official named Anne Rule, who would famously write The Stranger Beside Me about Bundy's life and his crimes. She claims that he was an empathetic and kind person who was effective in dealing for suicides that could be a possibility. He was, according to her extremely sensitive to those he spoke to and always seemed to be interested in the people on a personal level.

After 1972, Ted left politics and entered the fray in the reelection effort of the incumbent governor Daniel J. Evans. Ted was employed as an undercover agent by following Evans's opponents from location to location as well as recording the speeches of Evans's opponents. He also provided crucial information on Evans's opponents for his campaign. Following Evans's reelection, Ted was hired by the Washington State Republican Party as an assistant to Chairman, Ross Davis. Davis said that Davis described Bundy as a savvy and assertive person and as an individual with a "believed on the principles of the party." The year 1973 was the first time Bundy traveled to California. In California, he reconnected with Stephanie Brooks again. In awe of his newfound ambition and professional vigor, Stephanie restarted her relationship with Ted.

From that point on, Ted would maintain his relationship with both Brooks and Kloepfer. Due to their geographical separation and Ted's manipulative personality both women were unaware of the existence of the other. After being accepted into U.P.S.'s School of Law, Ted continued his relationship with Brooks. Brooks even flew in during the weekends to visit him, and he often introduced her to others who worked for him, such as his boss, Ross Davis, as his fiancée. They were talking about marriage, but suddenly, something happened that changed.

When he was in the month of January, couple of days from when Ted and Stephanie began to rekindle their romance He suddenly stopped communicating with his fiancée. The calls were ignored or dropped. The letters were not answered. It took until mid-February Stephanie to finally connect with Ted after which she finally spoke to Ted via phone. Stephanie obviously was angry with Ted. She demanded he explain to her why he quit talking to her and then why he was silent. Elizabeth was able to hear the conversation go still. Slowly and slowly, Ted responded. Ted spoke in a calm, steady voice

"Stephanie...I do not know what you're talking about."

He abruptly ended the call He then abruptly hung up, leaving Brooks in silence. They did not speak for the rest of their lives. Brooks has said that, in retrospect the entire experience was just Ted's way of retribution for breaking the ice with his girlfriend in the year 1968. What was Ted's reason?

"I simply wanted to demonstrate to myself that I was capable of having got married to her."

Then, Ted started skipping his law classes. Ted soon quit school for the last time. After that, across all over the Pacific Northwest, women one by one began disappearing.

First Blood

If it's about Bundy's list of victims his first killings are not certain. Due to his contradictory accounts to numerous journalist and biographers, and the less rigorous criminalology of the time there is no any definitive proof of Ted Bundy's crimes prior to 1970. Before his execution, he frankly admitted to numerous murders, but never gave any details. The kidnappings and murders that he admitted in or accused but never convicted of included:

* A kidnapping incident in the year 1969 that took place in Ocean City, New Jersey

* A pair of murders occurred in Atlantic City New Jersey, carried out while visiting family.

A 1972 murder took place in Seattle

A 1973 murder of a rider near Tumwater, Oregon

* A kidnapping in 1961 and the murder of a six-year old girl, at the time Bundy was just 14.

The first time we were able to confirm a violent act committed by Ted Bundy was in 1974 at the age of 27 years old. It is unclear if he killed at this time or not, Bundy attested that by at this point, he had developed the capability of committing crimes that included murder in a manner that was able to frighten the primitive forensic methods that were in use at the day.

It's January 1974. in the middle of the frigid Washington winter, when a person later identified as Bundy was able to break into the basement of 18-year-old University of Washington dance student Karen Sparks. After a quiet opening of her window the man carefully removed the rod of metal off her bed frame, while she lay in her bed, completely unaware. Looking down at the sleepy female, Bundy registered no emotion as he lifted the rod up above his head, then lowered it to her body, striking her several times on her head. Content that she was stunned, Bundy then sexually assaulted her with the rod. The sharp metal rod caused numerous internal wounds. Bundy was careful to conceal his identity before disappearing in the same way he came. The incident resulted in Sparks with permanent and severe brain injury. She was in a coma and then the remainder of her life was marked by severely disabled.

Ted's first fatal kill was a month after and was a eerie re-creation of Bundy's assault at Karen Sparks. Similar to Sparks, Lynda Anne Healey was a resident of a basement and was studying at UW. Bundy was probably aware of her prior to the incident due to her work at Radio station in the area which broadcasted weather conditions for skiers who were in the close Cascades. Ted tracked her down for a period of unknown time before he finally spotted her. The next night Ted waited outside for the right time. He could be noticed briefly by the roommates of Lynda who claimed to have seen an "shadow" in the window the night before. They fell asleep believing that it was just a dream. When they woke the next day, their roommate was absent.

In the dark, Bundy had snuck into Lynda's room , and bludgeoned she to death. After that, with her bed bleeding and he took the blue jeans, a blouse and a pair of boots from the closet of Lynda. The only thing they could find of her after the incident is her brain. Then, between Sparks and Healey who resided just 11 blocks away from one another and the surrounding neighborhoods of the campus were put on lockdown. Students, particularly female students did not go out in the evenings and closed their doors because they were afraid of what could occur to them. However, despite their cautions women were still disappearing in the hands of Ted Bundy. He was only beginning to get started.

The disappearances that would follow were frequent and disturbing. Each month, one young woman, identical in age and appearance like Bundy's two first victims, would vanish with out leaving a trace. In March, 19-year aged Donna Gail left her dormitory at Evergreen State College to go to a jazz show. She didn't make it to the show.

On the 17th of April Susan Elaine Rancourt disappeared on her way to a film. Like the victims before her, Elaine was a student in her case, Central Washington University. Bundy was working steadily to the south, and was now 110 miles to the south of Seattle.

On the 6th of May, Roberta Parks disappeared while on her way to a coffee meeting with a friend at the Student Union. She was studying in Oregon State University, Corvallis located 260 miles to the to the south of Seattle.

In June of this year, 22 , young Brenda Bell disappeared after leaving the Flame Tavern close to the airport of Seattle-Tacoma International. One of the first instances of what would later be known as Bundy's mo, she was last heard talking to a man with brown hair who was slinging his arm around wrapped around his strap.

Bundy's second murder at Bundy's next killing in Northwest occurred in his personal backyard and killed the body of a UW student known as Georgann Hawkins. Contrary to previous killings that were committed, the disappearance of Hawkins was ablaze in a well illuminated alleyway that was between her boyfriend's residence and her sorority residence.

A developing MO

As the murder of Lynda Healey and the attack at Karen Sparks sent their small neighborhood in Seattle in a state of panic,

Bundy's bloody stretch across the northwest was the largest source of terror throughout the region during the period. The police departments of areas where women were missing scrambled to locate something or something that could be used to link to the unidentified killer. Due to the meticulous execution of Bundy of his crimes, investigators faced a dearth of evidence. In the case of Georgann Hawkins three detectives as well as an forensic scientist searched the area where she went missing. They found nothing. The limited information that was circulated by the media caused a flurry of fear in the hearts of people from Oregon or Washington. Not only were the standard security measures of locked doors and unofficial curfews into place but also hitchhiking especially by women (still extremely frequent in the early 70's) saw a drastic decline.

The only evidence the police had weren't disclosed to the media and only the tiniest amount of information being released because they were afraid that making it public could affect their investigation. Even with their limited evidence, they were able to gain an understanding of the method of operation used by Bundy.

Prior to this all disappearances occurred in the evening. They all occurred near examination time, when a large portion of the students would be too focused on their studies to take note of anything unusual happening. The victims were all females with hair that was dark. All of them were wearing blue jeans or slacks. In addition, it was evident in each crime scene, eyewitness account that the same person was seen in the vicinity prior to the disappearance. From the time of Donna Gail in March, the man with brown hair was observed with his arms in the sling, driving an orange Volkswagen Beetle. At times, he identified himself as Ted or Ted, and was often soliciting help to move a large object that was in his car such as books or bags or other.

He would keep a powerful weapon, often such as a crowbar within reach once he and his victim reached the vehicle. When he got them to in the location he wanted then they would be beaten and then handcuff them in the car. At the end, the police would do all kinds of things to them that will differ depending on the victim. After they died they were stripped and he would put their bodies into a distant location. Later, he would donate their clothing to charitable organizations, most often Goodwill. Ted was now a full accomplished serial killer and was only beginning to get started. The police used a dark name to describe Bundy's victims list: the Girl of the Month Club which was named in reference to Ted's rate of work. From the time of the time of his arrest, Ted killed on average every month.

At the time of his day, Ted was working as an official at the Washington State Department of Emergency Services where he worked in the agency that was searching for, paradoxically, missing and missing women. He was in a relationship his relationship with Elizabeth Kloepfer yet again and was currently engaged to Carol Anne Boone, a couple who had divorced twice and had children.

Ted's final assault during his final attack in the Pacific Northwest happened on Sunday 14 July. His bravery had increased since the attack took place in the open air. The area he hunted was Lake Sammamish State Park, approximately 20 miles to the to the east from Seattle. Ted kept to his routine manner of conduct. In introducing himself as Ted with his arms in a sling , and speaking with an irritated accent the man asked women on the beach if could lend his hand to help with the sailboat he needed to remove from the back of his Volkswagen Beetle. Despite the small amount of information the media could provide on the beach, women were at a loss. Four women who he approached rejected him flatly. The fifth woman agreed to go along with him. They made it to their parking spot. After she saw the Volkswagen and couldn't spot any sailboats in sight and she sped off, she jumped.

He then contacted Janice Ott, a newlywed juvenile case worker who relocated to Seattle for work, but had left her husband in California. She had studied antisocial personality disorders at college and, ironicallyenough, was determined to assist people like Ted to beat their mental illness before it got too late. However, it turned out to be too late for her. The blonde 23 years old who was lonely and in search of her husband, was drawn to the handsome man who begged for assistance. When they reached Ted's Beetle and he managed to hold her in place and then put her inside his vehicle. She didn't die but. He had a different plan.

Ted was back at the beach, where his trap was set, but his bloodlust was wasn't satisfied. He was snooping around in the park, looking for the perfect victim. After Denise Naslund got up from an afternoon dinner with her husband and went into the restroom, Ted found his victim. A 5 foot 4 inch brunette who was studying to become a computer programmer. Denise left together with her puppy. The dog returned home alone. By dragging Denise into his vehicle or maybe knocking her out , and then drag her to the place, Ted drove off to his final destination. When he arrived, Ott watch as he mangled Naslund before her before proceeding to kill her also.

The incident at the lake eventually prompted the King County police to go to the public with information about Bundy's life and a composite sketch. Many of the people Bundy encountered during his time in Seattle identified the face of the man who was featured in all of the documents. Anne Rule, Ted's ex Elizabeth and Ted colleagues all came forward to blame Ted. However, due to the frenzied character of the incident as well as the magnitude of it police were bombarded with 200 or more tips per day. Bundy is a beautiful young law student who had no criminal history, did not check all the boxes of an investigation into a spree killer.

Two hunters in September discovered two skeletons along an unpaved road that is 2 miles away from Sammamish as well as an additional femur as well as several vertebrae. Six months later university students discovered their victims' skulls in the east of the forest of Issaquah. However, by the time the entire thing was found, Ted was long gone. He was now moving to the to the east with gore and blood on the ground.

Bundy The Mountain Bundy The Mountains

Ted Bundy was a driven man who was confident of his own intellect and aspired to be successful. Therefore, in 1974 Ted Bundy decided to try a new chance at law school. In the past, when he had applied and was accepted, he'd been accepted by both the University of Puget Sound and the University of Utah. At that time, he had decided to transfer to UPS in order to be active in local politics as well as manage his girlfriends.

On his second attempt, Ted didn't want to remain in close proximity. He was already in hot water with the police following the release of the police sketch and he did not want to be a part of the murders he committed. When he was offered another acceptance from the University of Utah Law School He jumped at the opportunity. He packed his possessions and relocated from Seattle to Salt Lake City. Elizabeth Kloepfer, his on again off again girlfriend who was recently back with Ted was left in Seattle. They kept in touch over the phone, but Ted was not devoted to Elizabeth. According to his own account the attractive and beautiful Bundy was a frequent visitor to a number of women and was allegedly still being with Elizabeth in a long-distance relationship.

However, despite the opportunity that he received from attending law school for the second time, Ted ran into a blockage fairly quickly. The course he was required to study in the first time in his law school was almost unintelligible to Ted. The classes were too challenging according to him and his fellow students were he believed had an advantage over him both academically and intellectually. When describing his feelings regarding the events of this week, Ted declared it a failure. It's a bit of an understatement considering how his displeasure at the circumstances could result in.

Ted could not just walk away from his violent impulses and it wasn't long before his anger with law school turned to violence again.

The first time he was killed, he was in Idaho and he preyed on the driver of a hitchhiker. There is no information about this victim other than that Bundy assaulted and strangled her before dragging her away into the wild. He returned the following day with a camera snapping pictures as he dismembered the body , before throwing the body parts into the nearby river. They weren't ever recovered.

His first known kill at this time of his career came from Nancy Wilcox, on October 2nd. In contrast to his other kills until this point or at the very least, those we can confirm from, Nancy wasn't in college , or even at the age of college. While she was in to his "type" of brunettes who were young however, she was only 16 and attending high school when she died. She was abducted by Bundy in the suburb of Holladay and was last seen with a bug like the one that was confirmed to be Bundy's prior to her disappearance. She was driven into the woods in a quiet area where he was planning to raped her and then let her go. According to Bundy was a plot to ward off his lust for violence. However, it wasn't over.

The screams of Nancy, who was obviously terrified, were heard throughout the forest, and Bundy immediately acted to calm her.

He wrapped his arms around her throat and squeezed her. As Bundy's memories show the incident was not a plot to kill her. However, whether he did so intentionally or not Bundy's grip became too tight and he was holding it for too long, and Nancy Wilcox quickly was strangled to death. The body was buried in a patch of forest 200 miles to the south of location from which he had taken her, in an area located near an area that is isolated Capitol Reef National Park. Despite Bundy's confirmation of the burial site, authorities did not find any trace from Nancy Wilcox.

Then he decided to pursue Melissa Smith, the 17 year young niece of Chief Police of Midvale, Utah. Similar to Holladay Midvale was a tiny town of tight-knit Mormons that served as a suburb of Salt Lake City. In a town that was safe like that, with her father serving as the chief, 5'3 Melissa probably had no anxiety walking around her tiny town at any time. However, on October 18th of 1975, the situation changed. The next night, she planned to visit a friend's home for the night. She stopped by in a pizza restaurant to comfort the friend who'd been in an argument with their boyfriend, before heading home to pick up her clothes for the night and toiletries out of her house. The woman never made it to the store. Her body was discovered nine days later, naked , and with evidence of sexual assault strangulation, and sodomy. The bruises and gashes that covered her body were caused by repeatedly beatings with the Crowbar. A postmortem examination revealed that the 17-year-old was alive for seven days prior her death. Prior to the funeral, Bundy detailed the strange procedure he performed using Smith's body. When she died He began to offer her what could be described as a transformation. He washed, brushed and cut her hair, which was getting tangled after a fighting and matted with blood. Her body was discovered in the Wasatch Mountain just ten days after she disappeared.

The same murder took place just two weeks after Melissa's death. 17-year-old Laura Aime was brunette like Melissa but was taller and extremely thin. A high school dropout who was insecure She was a drifter and worked odd jobs in Lehi, Utah before

Bundy took her. She went to a cafe at night on Halloween and left around midnight to go for a walk. There was no chance in the murder of Aime. He was systematically brutally raped, tortured, and beat her using a crowbar before swiftly and calmly killing her using a pair of nylon stockings. As with the remains that was Melissa Smith, Aime's corpse was repeatedly beaten post mortem, and she was decorated with cosmetics and shampoo. Her body was discovered at the time of Thanksgiving Day, in a uninteresting canyon that was nine miles to the to the north Lehi.

A few days later, Ted Bundy made his first mistake of a major nature. The victim in question was an 18-year-old phone operator by the name of Carol Daronch. She ran into Bundy in the at the mall. She was there to see her cousins and left them to purchase a book from Walden's Books. Walden's Books. Then, a handsome young man wearing uniform suited for police walked up to her in the middle of the aisle. This was a brand new strategy for Bundy who up to now relied on his attractive appearance and natural charisma to attract clients. In some instances, however, the usual ruse of an injured person in need of assistance wouldn't be enough. Therefore, he utilized his passion for authority to make himself appear as an authority figure, typically such as a firefighter or policeman. In this disguise that he enticed Carol Daronch back to his vehicle, which was a light brown Volkswagen according to Ted's typical preference. He explained to her that somebody had broken into her vehicle and that she had to go with him to inspect the vehicle and fill out some forms. While she was skeptical, Bundy was able to overcome any defenses. When she got to her car that was unharmed and no missing items, Daronch asked questions. While he was still putting on a show, Ted then told her she must go "to the police station" to find out who the suspect was. She walked along with him until they reached the rear of a building. He claimed it was an office, but it was actually an unwashed laundry. There was no suspect, nor police on the scene, Bundy had to spin his wheels to stop Daronch from further questioning. Bundy had his own mark in his grasp however his cover was rapidly unravelling. He chose to move the story forward by citing an imagined "headquarters" to be the location in which his suspect lived. This is how he got her inside the Volkswagen. Once she was inside she was just enough of the "policeman" for him to detect the alcohol in his breath. Inquiring about things and the thought of an officer driving the Bug eventually sparked Daronch's survival instincts in high level. But, when her time came to leave, Ted was already speeding off at high speed. He advised her to buckle her seat belt on, and she realised that they were traveling, not towards the police headquarters but away from it.

The cover was now completely over, Ted hit his brakes and the car slammed to a stop. Profiting from Daronch's confused state after the abrupt stopping, Ted lunged over and attempted to cuff her. In a flurry of instinct, Daronch broke out of her stupor and swiftly engaged her captor. In such a tiny car, Daronch put up enough for a fight that she was able to knock Ted off. He committed the fatal error when he put both cuffs on one wrist. With her hand unblocked and his bounds now in a state of tense, Ted had to appeal to violence that was baldfaced. In grabbing a pistol small from his jacket He threatened to shoot her if she did not leave the scene. Unfazed, Daronch fell out of the car. While she lay in the mud with a mild rain was falling on her face She noticed the dark-skinned figure in the form of Ted Bundy emerge from the car. He held a crowbar on his palm.

She tried to get away from him but the dense mud made it difficult to get away. The little girl was picked up and then slammed her against the side of the vehicle. In a flash of adrenaline triggered by her survival instincts she broke free again. She began running along the road at an unrestrained pace, disregarding the rain and mud, and any other debris that was underfoot. She walked out into the street with Ted close behind her. With her adrenaline drained, Daronch sat at the side of the road , praying she would be able to get someone else. Luckily, they did. A couple from the past approached the intersection and saw a tiny woman with mud all over her face by on the other side. The couple took her astonishment as factual the couple slid Daronch in their car. They drove off, placing Bundy in the rear as fast as they could. Carol Daronch became the first to survive Ted Bundy who could attest to his identity and strategy. She was a crucial source for the current multi-state manhunt.

Bundy was slunking away, angry up and then irritated. The bloodlust of Bundy had not been satisfied however, he'd also been defeated. Bundy wasn't a person who was happy to be outwitted or even beaten. Therefore, he drove north, wallowing in a violent rage while he sought out another victim. He discovered that he had been released from Viermont High School, 19 miles to the north of his mishap to Carol Daronch. The victim was 17-year old Debby Kent who was at the play alongside her family. Her brother was skating at the local ice arena and it was her duty to collect him at the end of the play. When she left her parents in the house to rest, she went out. She didn't come back and her brother didn't see her in the ice rink. Students and the drama teacher also report an unknown person asking them to find the car that was broken into. One student claimed to have seen the same man outside the school, who was pacing in a hurry. However, the students in the school were unaware of the reports. They even were able to hear screams and loud screams from a person they described as filled with "mortal horror." Some students were even seen looking out at the darkening night and saw nothing. As the number of people at the school dwindled and the clock was getting toward midnight, Debbie's parents as well as brother became increasingly irritable. When the time was right for midnight the parents, who were angry, walked out from the theater and waited at the curb. However, when they saw that the parking lot was empty, with only one car in their vehicle, they realized that something was wrong. They phoned the police. Police officers were already worried following the many disappearances, deaths and disappearances in the towns around. They quickly establish an investigation scene and search for clues. They only found the key to the handcuffs Carol Daronch was wearing when she arrived in Murray, Utah. Murray,

Utah police station. Debby Kent was not discovered as well as Bundy never lied about her final resting spot.

Elizabeth Kloepfer, Ted's ex-girlfriend whom he'd left during her move staying on top of his activities. She listened to the news about disappearances but was still aware of Ted's previous actions during his stay in Washington. She contacted to the King County police again. After having had the time to look into the matter, as they'd dismissed Bundy as suspect, they had moved him higher up the suspects list. Unfortunately, their most reliable witness to Bundy's murders in Lake Sammamish did not identify Bundy as the murderer in the photo list. Then, in December of last year, she contacted to the Salt Lake County Sheriff's office and provided her information to them. They also didn't find enough information to tie Bundy to the latest string of disappearances. For the moment, Bundy was safe. In the beginning of 1975, following his final exam and a trip to Seattle for one time with Kloepfer. There was no mention of her relationship with the police.

However, they had plans to travel to Utah later in the year.

Ted knew that the heating was on again and he was especially concerned about Daronch's escape. Therefore, while he was at Salt Lake City to continue his law degree and pursue his murders, he transferred them into Utah's neighbour to the East, Colorado.

Ted's first murder in Colorado was almost immediately following the time his departure from Seattle. The victim was a 23-year old nurse Caryn Campbell who was engaged to marry and planning her wedding. When Ted took heraway, she was going on a ski excursion with her fiance as well as his two children of his prior marriage. After an exhausting day of mountain skiing they sat in the lounge at the lodge for a relaxing time after dinner. Caryn was suffering from an illness at the time was able to leave a magazine within their bedroom. She didn't return. In the wake of the absence of her partner set out to find her. Despite his furious search through the room and lodge but she was nowhere to be found. The last time he saw her was until her corpse was found on an unpaved roadway just from the ski area. She was repeatedly raped before being killed using the blunt instrument which caused a skull crease the place it hit. She was also injured repeatedly by a weapon that was sharp.

In the month of March 1975 Bundy was again killed with another fatality in Vail, Colorado, a town situated 100 miles north of the place where he'd murdered Caryn Campbell. Julie Cunningham was a 26 year old instructor of skis who worked in the store for sporting goods. He was with her while she was headed to a dinner out with a pal. He walked up to her on crutches, requesting help in putting his ski boots in his car. When they reached the vehicle, he kicked her on the head and then handcuffed her. Then , she drove 90 miles towards Rifle, Colorado, where she was raped and then strangled her, just like previously done to the other victims. Contrary to previous of victims Bundy was not content to decay where she was left. He returned to examine Cunningham's remains Cunningham after a couple of weeks and drive for six hours away from Salt Lake City. Again despite Bundy's confession, and confirmation of the burial location the body of Julie Cunningham was never recovered.

Denise Oliverson disappeared a month later on April 6th at Grand Junction, Colorado, near the border between Colorado and Utah. The 25-year old was headed to her parents' home after an argument between her and her partner. All they found of her was a bicycle and sandals beneath a bridge close to the railway.

Conclusion

The majority of people who are not in their twenties or were not old enough to be able to recall the brutality of Bundy's actions against humanity are unable to comprehend why a human being who could function independently might be unable to feel empathy and a conscience which would allow the committing of such crimes. Bundy during his last days of confessing to his actions and describing the circumstances that influenced on his actions was able to talk about his childhood and its less than ideal situations - like having no idea of his biological father and inability to connect with others during the time during adolescence, in which people are very social. For those who are analyzing the early life of Bundy it is apparent that the situation he was forced to play came with its fair own set of challenges, however nothing so troubling as it could explain his sociopathic inclination to the path of violence he pursued. When his initial murder spree was over in the Seattle neighborhood, people who were close to Bundy began to suspect that the brilliant, articulate law student could be the gruesome killer whose picture was being circulated by the police. Authorities themselves believed that he was not clean and well-educated enough to go so far that he would brutally assault victims with objects that were blunt while they lay asleep, only to continue to assault women sexually, and then return to have a sex session in their dead bodies, which he then left to decay. However, even after authorities managed to prove the evidence needed that justified arresting and bringing the suspect on trial, they were unable to comprehend his insanity as he amazingly managed two escapes, the third crucial when he again tried to satisfy his desire to murder. This would be the last of his series of murders committed by young women who he'd never had the pleasure of meeting, and each of whom was taken away from friends and family in the midst in their life. Bundy's need for control could be his downfall, as he was able to refuse a plea bargain that would have ensured your life saved even if behind bars for the majority of the remainder of his existence. Instead, he put his destiny in the care an Florida judge, who gave him the death penalty. The final days of his life also included confessions of murder that bring to an end the story of many victims, giving their families satisfaction and peace of mind that knowing the reason for their deaths could bring. His execution on the 24th of January 1989, was openly applauded by those who supported the death penalty, as well as those who argued for an eye-for-eye approach to justice however, it was not so than jubilantly acclamated by those whose lives were not filled by what he knowingly took from the other victims was taken away from his own.

www.ingramcontent.com/pod-product-compliance
Lightning Source LLC
Chambersburg PA
CBHW050025130526
44590CB00042B/1909